VAULT CAREER GUIDE TO CONSULTING

© 2007 Vault Inc.

VAULT CAREER GUIDE TO CONSULTING

LAURA WALKER CHUNG, ERIC CHUNG
AND THE STAFF OF VAULT

© 2007 Vault Inc.

Copyright © 2007 by Vault Inc. All rights reserved.

All information in this book is subject to change without notice. Vault makes no claims as to the accuracy and reliability of the information contained within and disclaims all warranties. No part of this book may be reproduced or transmitted in any form or by any means, electronic or mechanical, for any purpose, without the express written permission of Vault Inc.

Vault, the Vault logo, and "The Most Trusted Name in Career Information™" are trademarks of Vault Inc.

For information about permission to reproduce selections from this book, contact Vault Inc., 150 W. 22nd St., 5th Floor, New York, NY 10011, (212) 366-4212.

Library of Congress CIP Data is available.

ISBN 10: 1-58131-531-7

ISBN 13: 978-1-58131-531-8

Printed in the United States of America

The media's wat
Here's a samplir

....

"Unflinching, fly-on-the-wall r
propaganda to the nitty-gritty inside dope better than these guys."
— *Knight-Ridder newspapers*

"Best way to scope out potential employers...Vault has sharp insight into corporate culture and hiring practices."
— *Yahoo! Internet Life*

"Vault has become a de facto Internet outsourcer of the corporate grapevine."
— *Fortune*

"For those hoping to climb the ladder of success, [Vault's] insights are priceless."
— *Money.com*

"Another killer app for the Internet."
— *New York Times*

"If only the company profiles on the top sites would list the 'real' information... Sites such as Vault do this, featuring insights and commentary from employees and industry analysts."
— *The Washington Post*

"A rich repository of information about the world of work."
— *Houston Chronicle*

ACKNOWLEDGMENTS

We are extremely grateful to Vault's entire staff for all their help in the editorial, production and marketing processes. Vault also would like to acknowledge the support of our investors, clients, employees, family and friends. Thank you!

Table of Contents

INTRODUCTION 1

THE SCOOP 3

The Basics of Consulting 5
What is Consulting? 5
Consulting Skill Sets 11
The Traveling Salesman Problem 14
Who Hires Consultants, and Why? 17
Industry History and Trends 19
Current Trends 20
Consulting Versus Other Career Paths 27

Consulting Categories 31
Types of Consulting Services 31
Types of Firms 39

GETTING HIRED 47

Targeting Consulting Firms 49
Researching Companies, the Right Way 49
Interviewing the Consultants 56

The Hiring Process 59
The Recruiting Process: An Overview 59
Tailoring Your Resume for Consulting 60
How to Strengthen a Non-Business Resume 61
Sample Resumes and Cover Letters 64
Building and Maintaining a Network 72
Applying to the Firm 74
Lateral Hires 77

The Interview 81
What to Expect in the Interview 81

The Resume/Behavioral Interview 82
Behavioral Questions 83
Practice Behavioral Interview Questions 83
The Case Interview 85
Sample Qualitative Case Questions 88
Guesstimates 92
Sample Guesstimate 93
More Sample Guesstimates 94
Brainteasers 94
Sample Brainteasers 95
Practicing with Your Friends Before the Interview 96
Questions for the Interviewer 99
Interview Questions that Never Get Asked .99
Behavior 101

Post-Interview: Accepting, Negotiating, Declining 103

After the Interview 103
Accepting an Offer 104
Negotiating an Offer 105
Turning Down an Offer 107
What to Do When Things Don't Work Out .109

ON THE JOB   113

The Project Life Cycle   115
The Project Life Cycle 115

Tips for High Performance   121
Troubleshooting 121
How to Survive Your First Month on the Job 125
Getting Staffed 131
On the Beach 132

The Consulting Career Path   137
Training for Consultants 137
Consulting Job Descriptions and Career Progression 138

Mentors: Top-Level Backing 148
Exit Strategies 149

Our Survey Says: The Consulting Lifestyle   151

Diversity Issues in Consulting: State of the Industry 159

Days in the Life   163

Associate 163
Consultant Project Manager 165
MBA-Level Strategy Consultant 168
IT Strategy Consultant 172

CONCLUSION   175

APPENDIX   177

Industry Buzzwords 179
About the Authors 184

How many consulting job boards have you visited lately?

(Thought so.)

Use the Internet's most targeted job search tools for consulting professionals.

Vault Consulting Job Board

The most comprehensive and convenient job board for consulting professionals. Target your search by area of consulting, function, and experience level, and find the job openings that you want. No surfing required.

VaultMatch Resume Database

Vault takes match-making to the next level: post your resume and customize your search by area of consulting, experience and more. We'll match job listings with your interests and criteria and e-mail them directly to your inbox.

Introduction

Your dream job?

Love the idea of jetting to locations both exotic and banal and getting paid very well for your intellectual capital? A lot of consultants (current and prospective) do, too.

Management consulting continues to rank among the most popular professions for emerging MBAs and college graduates, and for good reason. As one of the better-paid professions for recent graduates, consulting offers lucrative salary packages and the chance to meet elite Fortune 500 managers. Moreover, consultants get to work on high-level strategic decisions for their clients—certainly some of the most interesting issues in business management today.

But consulting careers are no walk in the park: Pressures are high, travel can be onerous, the interview process can be painful, the work content isn't always glamorous, and job security is low relative to many other professions. Before setting off on the consulting route too enthusiastically, you need to get a sense of how you might like it. This requires an understanding of where the industry is going, your role in the industry, and how closely it fits with your needs and personality.

You may have picked up this guide in an attempt to decide whether or not consulting is for you. We suggest you start your journey by doing a personal inventory of your skills and talents, as well as your interests and sources of intellectual satisfaction. Also, find out about other professionals' experiences—both the war stories and the rewards. If your network doesn't include other consultants, use the message boards on Vault's consulting channel or join an industry organization for leads. And read this guide to see if consulting really interests you.

This book is not meant to pump up consulting. Rather, it's meant to be a reality check to give you a practical understanding of what consulting is really like. If you decide it's for you, the top-notch advice you'll find in this guide will give you the best shot of breaking in.

Just remember that positions are limited, and competition ranks among the highest of many industries. Even if you attended a top-five MBA program or have decades of experience, breaking into consulting requires perseverance and the sharpest of networking and persuasion skills. Furthermore, consulting firms tend to hire disproportionately from the so-called top schools. One third of grads from the most prestigious MBA programs join a consulting firm, while just a small fraction of those from lower-ranked MBA programs make it into the industry. And, the skew toward higher-ranked schools is equally true for undergraduate institutions.

No matter where your school ranks and no matter where you are in your professional career, this guide will help give you a shot at one of these coveted positions. The road to consulting is challenging; the potential rewards, however, are great.

THE SCOOP

Chapter 1: The Basics of Consulting

Chapter 2: Consulting Categories

The Basics of Consulting

CHAPTER 1

What is Consulting?

A giant industry, a moving target

Consultants offer skill in assessing and solving business problems, and are hired by companies who need their expertise, fresh outside perspective, and/or extra set of hands. Some management consulting firms specialize in giving advice on general business strategy questions, while others are known as technology, marketing, finance, operations or human resources specialists. Some concentrate on a specific industry area, like financial services or retail, and still others are more like gigantic one-stop shops with divisions that dispense advice on everything from top-level strategy, to choosing customer account management software, to saving money on paper clips.

But consulting firms have one thing in common: they run on the power of their people. The only product consulting firms ultimately have to offer is their employee's ability to make problems go away. As a consultant, you are that problem-solver.

Not the kind of consulting we mean

As a stand-alone term, "consulting" lacks real meaning. In a sense, everyone's a consultant. Have you ever been asked by a friend, "Do I look good in taupe?" Then you've been consulted for your color sense. There are thousands upon thousands of independent consultants who peddle their expertise and advice on everything from retrieving data from computers to house-training your new puppy. There are also fashion consultants, image consultants and wedding consultants.

This career guide covers a particular type of advisory work known as "management consulting" (and simply "consulting" as the conventional, but confusing, shorthand). Management consulting involves nontechnical consulting to the senior management of private- and public-sector organizations. We do not include computer programming, systems integration or other kinds of technical outsourcing—this, of course, is also a version of consulting (and an extremely large industry that employs many new graduates), but we won't discuss it in this book.

Management consulting firms, then, sell business advisory services to the leaders of corporations, governments and nonprofit organizations. Typical functional concentrations in consulting include strategy, information technology (IT), human resources (HR), finance, marketing and operations. Types of problems in consulting might include developing an improved service marketing plan, pulling together a strategy for a new product launch, planning for technology investments inside the client firm, valuing external investments from a financial perspective or evaluating the impacts of a government policy. Consulting firms sell services in virtually any industry, such as pharmaceuticals, consumer packaged goods, heavy manufacturing, high tech or energy.

Consulting firms are typically organized or broken up according to industry and type of problem as well. For example, a firm might focus on strategy problems only, but in virtually any industry. Bain & Company is an example of one such firm. Another firm might focus on just a specific industry, but advise on nearly any type of issue. Oliver Wyman, which focuses on the financial services industry, is an example of this type of firm. Many of the larger firms have a "matrix" organization, with both industry practice groups and functional practice groups. And some firms are extremely specialized. For example, a firm might have only two employees, both focusing solely on competitive analysis in the telecommunications industry. All of these are examples of management consulting.

Caveats about consulting

All this might sound great, but before we go on, we should provide a few reality checks regarding the experience of a consulting career:

It takes a long time before you are having meetings with CEOs— Outsiders sometimes imagine a 23-year-old hotshot whispering words of wisdom into the eager ear of the chairman of the board. But, this scenario is as ludicrous as it sounds. Consulting does not often provide instant access to super-senior management. You won't be flying solo with your ideas until you're some 10 years post-MBA in the industry, and you may be working in a firm that never consults to C-level executives, but rather to line managers in marketing or operations. You'll be part of a project team of three to six consultants, with a partner in charge, and possibly active team members from the client company as well. There will be a clear hierarchy, with seniority-appropriate tasks doled out amongst the players, and an expectation that everyone works transparently and collaboratively. It's through a healthy dose of down-in-the-ditches research, painstaking analysis and thoughtful communication that you'll persuade your client to change how she does business. There's no wizard who sits on the CEO's shoulder.

Consulting is glamorous only once in a while—Consulting can indeed be exciting and high profile, but this is the exception, not the rule. Chances are, you won't be sitting across from the CEO at your next project kick-off, and you probably won't be staying in four-star hotels in the coolest cities around the world (though both are indeed possible). Your day-to-day experience might very well be sleeping in a Travelodge motel, eating at Applebee's, and working with a grumpy middle-manager who didn't ask for your firm to be there. But that's OK, because glamour has little to do with how interesting your project is, and most consultants love their jobs for the intellectual challenge.

Consulting is prestigious in only certain circles—Consulting is widely thought of as a prestigious career within business circles, and particularly among MBAs. But you should realize that in contrast to work in investment banking, your work in consulting will probably never get mentioned in *The Wall Street Journal*. Very few consulting firms are publicly recognized for the help they give, and most "civilians" won't have heard of your firm at all. Furthermore, consulting clients usually require their service providers to sign a confidentiality agreement, and you therefore won't be able to tell your friends or family which client firm you are working for, or discuss the details of your latest fascinating project.

Few people outside of the industry really understand what consulting is, how many tough hours you put into your job, or how much effort and talent is required to sustain a successful consulting career. In fact, a running joke about consulting is that no one can explain it to outsiders, no matter how hard or how many times one tries. If you want a job you can concretely explain to your grandparents, or one that always generates an approving nod from non-business folks, consulting isn't for you.

Consulting is unlikely to make you rich—The salary looks attractive on paper, but you should understand that it's neither easy money nor a truly lucrative income. Divide your salary over the (large) number of hours, and the pay per hour is often well below that of other business careers. Many consultants early in their careers calculate that their hourly wages are similar to those in a retail sales or barista position. In other words, unless you make it to a partner position, where income jumps up dramatically, consulting won't make you rich. In any case, we strongly urge everyone to avoid pursuing any career based on income expectations—that is a career planning approach likely to lead to dissatisfaction and unhappiness in the end.

Being a good consultant is much harder than you think—You might be thinking, "All consultants do is figure out what problems companies have, explain them, and move on." That's pretty much never true. Spotting a client's problems is a mere fraction of the battle. Most people with a fair amount of common sense and an outsider's perspective can identify a client's problems. And in many cases, clients also understand where the problems lie.

The job of the consultant isn't just about knowing what's wrong. It's about figuring out how to make it right. Even finding the solution and making a quality recommendation isn't necessarily the end of the story. Consultants must make sure the solution isn't too expensive, impractical or politically difficult to implement. Many consulting firms have what's called an 80 percent solution: It's better to put in place a solution that takes care of 80 percent of the problem than to strive for a perfect solution that can't be put into place. Consultants must also get buy-in from the clients. Not only does bureaucracy often make implementation tough, but consultants must also convince individual client employees to help them make solutions work. It's tough to solve problems, and that's why clients hire consultants.

So what does a consultant actually do, anyway?

Most non-consultants are mystified by the actual job and its day-to-day responsibilities. There are good reasons why this is so. While you're used to giving advice and solving problems, you may not understand how this translates into a career path. The problem is compounded because consultants tend to use a very distinctive vocabulary. You may not know what it means to think outside the box, what the point of taking a 50,000-foot view is, or why consultants keep talking about frameworks when they don't know the first thing about how to build a house. In addition, many consulting firms have their own specific philosophies and problem-attacking methodologies, which only add to the jargon. (If you're stumped by this, check out the glossary at the end of this book.)

The short answer is that you will be working on projects of varying lengths at varying sites for different clients. What you do will depend on your seniority, experience, phase of the project and your company. If you are a partner, you are selling work most of the time, whereas if you have a recent MBA degree, you are probably overseeing a couple of entry-level consultants doing research. For the most part, we'll use this book to describe the job that entry-level (BA grads) and midlevel (first few years post-MBA) consultants do.

The Basics of Consulting

Generally, projects follow the cycle of pitching, research, analysis, reporting and implementation. You may also find yourself doing some administrative work throughout or after the project. Depending where you are in the project lifecycle, here are some of the things you could be doing:

Pitching

- Helping to sell and market the firm (preparing documents and researching prospective clients in preparation for sales calls that one of the senior managers or partners will make)
- Helping to write the project proposals (using PowerPoint and/or Word)
- Assisting in the presentation of a sales pitch to a prospective client

Research

- Performing secondary research on the client and its industry (using online company information databases like Bloomberg or Hoover's, periodical articles, SEC filings, client and competitor web sites, and general Internet searches)
- Interviewing the client's customers to gather viewpoints on the company
- Checking your firm's data banks for previous studies that it has done in the industry or with the client, and speaking to the prior project leaders about their insights on the client
- Facilitating or participating in a weekly client team discussion about the client company's business issues

Analysis

- Organizing and summarizing product or customer datasets in Excel, Access or SAS
- Conducting "back-of-the-envelope" or high-level summary calculations not requiring software
- Building quantitative financial models in Excel (depending on the project, an Excel model can be a one-hour task or a two-week task)
- Performing statistical analysis on data in Excel, SAS or SPSS
- Discussing the data, trends and preliminary model outputs with team members and supervisors
- Helping to generate insights and recommendations

Reporting

- Preparing interim, draft and final presentations (typically a "deck" of PowerPoint slides, though some firms write up longer reports in Microsoft Word format)
- Helping to present the findings and recommendations to the client, either via a conference call walk-through or in-person visual presentation

Implementation

- Acting as a project manager or "warm body" for the implementation of your strategy, if your firm is typically active during the implementation phase of a project
- Documenting a proposed process for the organizational change required to support the recommended strategy
- Documenting a proposed process for coding, systems integration and/or testing of the recommended system, if you work for an IT consulting practice
- Documenting the team's work after the project is over

Administration

- Working on internally-funded research when your firm has no billable projects for you
- Filling out weekly time tracking and expense reports

Keep in mind that the actual analysis phase—usually the most interesting part—is often the shortest part of a consulting assignment. Instead, consultants staffed on projects typically do a lot of research, Excel number crunching and (likely for the bulk of your time on the project) developing slides for a PowerPoint presentation. You will attend lots of meetings in your quest to find the data, create the process and meet the people who will help you resolve the issues you've been hired to address. And, when you're not staffed, you will spend time "on the beach" doing research on prospective clients and helping with marketing efforts. (It's called "on the beach" because the time when you're not staffed on a paid engagement is usually less frenetic—though not always so!) Consulting firms invest a lot of time in acquiring clients and securing project contracts. So, depending on how the firm is structured or how the economy is doing, you could spend significant amounts of time working on proposals. For you, this usually means lots of research, which is then elucidated on the omnipresent PowerPoint slides.

To some extent, though, the boundaries of the job are virtually limitless. Each project carries with it a new task, a new spreadsheet configuration, a new client team, new insights about business and economics, or a new challenge involving corporate culture and client office politics.

Consulting Skill Sets

As mentioned before, consultants focus their energies in a wide variety of practice areas and industries. Their individual jobs are as different as one could imagine. While an operations consultant may advise a client about lead times in their production facility, a technology consultant might create a training protocol for a new software package, and a marketing strategy specialist might think about how a new product will be received in China. What could be more different?

However, despite the big picture differences among types of management consulting, the day-to-day skill set required for all types of strategy projects is very consistent. It is worth your taking the time to think about if you possess or could develop in short order the attributes and abilities that would be highly valuable in consulting. We've assembled a list of some of the key skills below.

(Before we talk about the skill sets, keep in mind that there is a big difference between the job now and the job eight or so years after grad school, if and when you are a partner. We are going going to talk about whether you would like the job now, but at some point you should think about whether this might be a good long-term career for you. Is your goal to see it through to partner? If you seek an interesting job for a maximum five to six years, you only have to know you have the qualities to be a good consultant and manager. To be a partner, you have to be a persuasive strategic salesperson. You will spend nearly 100 percent of your time marketing expensive services to companies who sometimes don't think they need help. Your pay and job security will depend on your ability to make those sales.)

- **Do you work well in teams?** Consultants don't work alone. Not only do they frequently brainstorm with other consultants, but they also often work closely with employees at the client company, or even with consultants from other companies hired by the client. Consultants also frequently attend meetings and interview potential information sources. If you're the sort of person who only functions well in quiet, calm, structured environments, you will probably not enjoy being a consultant. (This, by the way, has nothing to do with your *preference*; it's more about your *ability* to take on the required team-oriented propensity of a consultant.)

- **Do you multitask well?** Not only can consulting assignments be frenetic, but consultants are often staffed on more than one assignment (though this varies significantly firm to firm). Superior organizational skills and a good sense of prioritization are your allies. Would your friends describe you as a really busy person who's involved in a ton of activities, and still able to keep your personal life on track? (There's the old saying: "If you want something done, get a busy person to do it.")

- **Speaking of friends, do you like talking to people?** Do you find yourself getting into interesting conversations over lunch and dinner? If you consider yourself a true introvert and find that speaking to people all day saps your energy, you will likely find consulting quite enervating. This doesn't mean that introverts don't make outstanding consultants; it means that introverts will likely find themselves tired in the evening from having been "on" all day. On the other hand, if you truly relish meetings, talking to experts, explaining your viewpoints, cajoling others to cooperate with you and making impromptu presentations, you'll slide into the job more easily from an interpersonal perspective.

- **Did you love school?** Did you really like going to class and doing your homework? There's a high correlation between academic curiosity and enjoyment of consulting. You should relish and be good at analysis and logical, structured thinking, as well as thinking creatively. Consultants must resolve ambiguous issues with hypothesis- or data-driven problem solving methods. (This is why people-oriented scientists can make great consultants.) You might already know that consultants have this expression called "thinking outside the box" that has invaded mainstream culture. This means the ability to find solutions not constrained by commonly accepted facts.

- **Are you very comfortable with numbers?** Consulting firms don't expect you to be a math professor, but you should be facile with figures, as well as competent with commonly used programs like Excel, Access and PowerPoint. When you go to the hair salon and pay your stylist $40 for a 30-minute cut, do you instinctively do the math on their implied annual income, accounting for downtime, vacation and fee splits with the salon? If you hate basic math, you will hate consulting.

- **Are you willing to work 70, even 80 hours a week?** Consultants must fulfill client expectations, and this often means burning the midnight oil.

Try working from 8 a.m. to 10 p.m. one day. Now imagine doing so five days a week for months on end (plus the occasional weekend day). Furthermore, imagine working that schedule into your 40s (in contrast to professions like medicine where initial hours are as bad as consulting, but usually drop to 40 hours or less per week after training ends). If you have rigid commitments outside 9-to-5 work hours, you may find consulting undesirable. New consultants quickly find that they need to approach dating, friendship, family obligations, vacations and extracurricular activities quite differently than "normal" people do. Season tickets to the symphony are a bad idea, as is a Thursday evening woodworking class. Vacations can get cancelled, no matter how far in advance you planned or how important it is to your parents that you join them for their anniversary. Live-in nannies are a must if you have children (unless you have a spouse who never works late and never travels). Even having pets requires special (and costly) accommodations for the consulting lifestyle. In fact, how would you do your dry cleaning if you haven't gotten out of the office on a weekday before 10 p.m. in a month? There's always a work-around, as long as you are willing to pay the financial and personal cost.

- **Last, but certainly not least, are you willing to travel frequently?** Will you be able to say an unqualified and enthusiastic "yes" to supervisor or client requests that you fly out tomorrow for three days at the last minute? Or, will you be the consultant who is always trying to negotiate less client-site time or always overusing conference calls to avoid in-person meetings? It's not only a question of whether you are willing to deal with the travel schedule, but whether you will be happy and fulfilled given such a schedule. (See the inset section for a discussion of the details of travel in consulting.)

Be truthful. If you can't answer most of these points with a resounding "yes," consulting is most likely not for you. The point is not just to get the job, but also to know what you're getting into—and to truly want to be a consultant. While the costs and requirements of consulting may seem outrageously high, the right person finds the rewards to be commensurate, and the career path to be extremely fulfilling.

The traveling salesman problem

A lot of people go into the consulting field with the notion that travel is fun. "Traveling four days a week? No problem! My last vacation to Vienna was a blast!" However, many soon find the traveling consultant's life to be a nightmare. Many consultants leave the field solely because of travel requirements.

Here's what we mean by consulting travel. Different consulting firms have different travel models, but there are two basic ones:

- A number of consulting firms (typically the larger ones) have policies that consultants spend four days per week on the client site, no matter what. This means traveling to the destination city Monday morning (or sometimes Sunday evening), spending three nights in a hotel near the client site, and flying home late Thursday night (or sometimes Friday morning instead). Firms usually try to staff "regionally" to reduce flying time for consultants, but that doesn't necessarily reduce the number of nights away from home.

- The other popular travel model is to go to the client site "as needed." This generally means traveling at the beginning of the project for a few days, at the end of the project for the presentation and a couple of times during the project for interim project updates. There is less regularity and predictability with this travel model (e.g., you don't figure out when you're traveling next week until the Friday before), but there is also less overall time on the road.

Here are some variations of these travel models that pop up frequently:

- International projects involve a longer-term stay on the client site. This is both because (1) there is so much inefficient air time involved and (2) flying consultants to and from the home country every week can get expensive. For example, the consultant might stay two or three weeks on or near the client site (the client might put you up in a corporate apartment instead of a hotel to save costs) and then go home for a week, repeating the process until the end of the project. Sometimes this works out OK—for example, we know of a consultant who happily flew his wife and newborn over from London to San Diego for a three-week stint in the winter. But it's usually a bit of a drag. Chances are you'll wind up hoping to trade in those long first-class flights to the Middle East for some quality time with your significant other, friends and family.

- Then, there is the "local" project that is really a long commute into a suburb, sometimes involving up to two hours in a car. Examples of this include consulting to Motorola (based in not-so-convenient Schaumberg, Ill.) while living in Chicago, consulting to a Silicon Valley client while living in San Francisco, or dealing with Houston traffic driving across town to work with Shell. In these cases, you might opt to stay at a local hotel after working late, instead of taking the long drive home. This is not very different from non-local travel, and it can be more grueling, due to the car commute.

You need to ask yourself a number of practical questions to see if you are travel-phobic. For example, when you pack to go on vacation, do you stress about it? Do you always underpack or overpack? Do you hate flying? Do you hate to drive? Do you mind sleeping in hotel rooms for long periods of time? Are you comfortable with the idea of traveling to remote cities and staying there for three or four nights every week for 10 weeks? If you're married, do you mind being away from your spouse (and children if you have them) for up to three nights a week? Does your family mind? Will your spouse understand and not hold it against you if you have to cancel your anniversary dinner because the client wants you to stay a day later? If you and your spouse both travel for work, who will take care of the pets? Does the idea of managing your weekly finances and to-do lists from the road bother you?

Sound silly? It isn't—welcome to the reality of the traveling consultant. If these questions make your stomach churn but you're still dead set on working as a management consultant, look for consulting situations that promise the strong potential for a more stable work environment. For example, if you focus on consulting to financial services institutions and live in New York City, most of your clients may be local. But consulting firms typically don't have the luxury of choosing their clients and their locations, so they can't guarantee you won't travel. If you absolutely cannot travel, some of the largest consulting firms, such as Accenture, do have specific business units that can guarantee a non-traveling schedule. Ask—but know that such positions tend to deal with internal and operational issues related to the consulting firm, not its clients. (You should also consider internal consulting divisions of large companies. We'll talk about such work environments in a later section.)

Note that travel is common in the consulting field, but not all consultants travel. And not all clients expect you to be on site all the time. It absolutely depends on the firm's travel model, industry, your location and, most importantly, your project. (See the following exhibit for illustrations of the potential travel models.)

Variation in travel requirements

As-needed travel policy: light travel

S	M	T	W	T	F	S
S	M	T	W	T	F	S
S	M	T	W	T	F	S
S	M	T	W	T	F	S

This consultant is currently staffed on a project where independent, desktop work is possible. He only travels for large group meetings at the client site that cannot be effectively handled by phone – and of course for the kickoff meeting and final presentation. His client is close enough geographically that sometimes day trips without an overnight stay are possible.

As-needed travel policy: heavy travel

S	M	T	W	T	F	S
S	M	T	W	T	F	S
S	M	T	W	T	F	S
S	M	T	W	T	F	S

This consultant has been staffed on a highly facilitative project where he needs to be on client site a lot. The client is overseas, which makes coming home for the weekend impractical. He is spending two weeks straight at the client site, alternating with one full week in his home office, for the duration of the project.

Always on client site policy

S	M	T	W	T	F	S
S	M	T	W	T	F	S
S	M	T	W	T	F	S
S	M	T	W	T	F	S

This consultant gets on a 6 a.m. flight every Monday morning without fail. Every Thursday night she flies back home by 11 p.m. and spends Friday in her own office, finishing up the week's project work remotely, as well as catching up on paperwork and other firm business.

☐ = out of town

Who Hires Consultants, and Why?

Corporations, governments, and nonprofit institutions hire consultants for a number of reasons. Every consulting project springs from a client's need for help, or at least the kind of help that short-term, internal hiring can't solve within the necessary timeframe. Some clients, for example, need to overhaul their entire IT infrastructure, yet they're out of touch with the latest back-end systems or don't have the staff resources for such a large project. Other clients may be merging, but lack any experience with post-merger staffing procedures and need a neutral party to mediate. Some clients may need an outsider's perspective on a plant shutdown. Perhaps a client wants to bring in extra industry knowledge or turnaround expertise, if it lacks the deep experience with financial and corporate restructuring that such experts can supply. Generally speaking, consultants are brought in because they can accomplish the task "better, faster and cheaper" than if the client was to do it alone.

(Don't get a big head about this. This doesn't mean that your clients are stupid in any way, shape or form just because they need you to help them. This is a very, very common trap that new consultants fall into. More than likely, your client contacts have more industry experience than you do and are your best resource for getting the information you need to structure and solve the problems. In fact, they often know the answer to the problem they've asked you to solve, and rather than go with their gut alone, they've hired you to be their extra set of eyes. For many companies, it's smart business practice to hire consultants to ensure a quality decision. This is a very important point—so important that we'll come back to it later in this book.)

Consultants might get hired for political reasons, too. Launching big projects can be very cumbersome, particularly at Fortune 500 companies. In order for a single dollar to be spent on such a project, most companies require senior executive approval. And without a major consultancy's brand name attached to the project, approval can be hard to get. But once a consulting firm steps into the picture, everyone involved has plausible deniability in the event that the project fails. There is an oft-repeated adage that "no one ever got fired for hiring McKinsey" (or a similarly prestigious consulting firm). Even though it's not true, some clients still cling to this statement as a rule of thumb.

But even if a giant project gets the green light, there's no guaranteeing it will be implemented. The reason? Bureaucratic inertia. Senior executives lose interest. Direct reports move on to other issues. In short, companies lose their focus. (Several years ago, an insider at a large private global corporation reported that action items from a 1996 BCG report had been approved, but as of 2002, had not yet been implemented.) By bringing in consultants to oversee large projects, companies ensure that someone is always watching the ball. In many cases, the correct solution may be quite evident to many, but having it confirmed by an outside party makes implementing a plan easier politically.

In an era of downsizing, consultants have another political use. Companies with an itch to fire a percentage of their workforce could prefer to bring in consultants. When the consultants recommend a workforce reduction, the company can fire at will, blaming their hired guns for the downsizing.

For many types of companies, consultants are a form of cost-effective labor. It costs the firm less money to hire outsiders to help them with a project, rather than hire some folks full-time at the expense of a competitive salary and benefits package. Consultants may also get the job done in a shorter timeframe, not because they are necessarily more efficient, but because the company might not get away with forcing regular employees to adhere to a compressed time frame by working the late hours consultants will. Good consultants will bring in a fresh, results-oriented approach to a client environment, completing projects at a pace that is usually much faster than that of the client's workforce.

Whatever the reasons for hiring consultants, they're bound to be compelling—because, even despite the cost-effectiveness argument, consultants are very costly. Excluding travel expenses and actual project fees, hourly prices for even midlevel consultants can easily climb into the $300-500 per hour range.

The worker behind the curtain

Consultants are a back-room breed of professional. In joint projects with their clients, they do much of the work and can expect little of the recognition. All consultants must deliver bottom-line value, and often spend countless hours huddled in cramped spaces to do just that. If you do a great job, your client will thank you, but you may never hear about it again. In some cases, you will leave your project before its completion and may never know whether it succeeded or failed.

If you enjoy recognition, a sense of completion and long-term relationships, you will want to consider the type of consulting firm you join. Does your firm have a history of repeat business? If so, you will have a better chance of seeing the client through different projects and business cycles; you may even work with the same client on different engagements. (Marakon Associates, for example, boasts that 90 percent of its work comes from engagements with previous clients.) Other firms might offer a methodology that isn't as repeatable. If your firm focuses solely on competitive analysis studies, chances are good that, if your client stays in the same industry, you won't need to sell that service to them again for a while.

Economic consulting firms like CRA International often help law firms with litigation support, including research, economic analysis and testimonies. This can be very interesting work, and since you're supporting one side or the other of a public dispute, you will certainly know how the fruits of your labor will turn out. Depending on the size of the dispute, so might everyone else who follows the business news.

Another example is M&A consulting. Some firms, like L.E.K. Consulting, have practice areas specifically focused on due diligence, company analysis, and transaction support. The bad news is that on such projects, you are subject to the even longer and more erratic hours suffered by other M&A professionals. On the bright side, you will eventually read in *The Wall Street Journal* about any triumph enjoyed by your client. Your consulting firm may not be mentioned, but at least you will be able to see the results of your hard work become a reality. (It'll also be easier for you to transition to working in the financial industry in the future, if that is your wish.)

So, think about the level of recognition, sense of closure and focus on relationship-building you need to be fulfilled by your work, and look for a firm that does the type of work that suits your needs.

Industry History and Trends

A brief history of consulting

People have traded wisdom for pay since the dawn of time. Nonetheless, consulting as big business only came into being around the start of the 20th century.

The first consultants drew from their engineering backgrounds to conduct projects for their clients. Arthur D. Little is widely recognized as the first such firm, founded in 1886 in Cambridge, Massachusetts. Booz Allen Hamilton was established in the early 20th century with a similar structure.

The trend continued when James "Mac" McKinsey, a University of Chicago professor, established his "accounting and engineering advisors" firm in 1926, offering a proposition similar to consulting. Over time, he developed a unique, integrated approach for his clients, which he called his "general survey." Instead of hiring traditional engineers, he recruited experienced executives and trained them in a framework of analysis. The new approach considered goals, strategies, policies, organization, facilities, procedures and personnel. In the late 1950s, a number of other consulting firms emerged with focused strategies and novel frameworks.

A notable innovator, The Boston Consulting Group (BCG), developed the experience curve. The experience curve proposed that declines in most industries were directly correlated to cost as a function of cumulative experience. BCG later extended its original concept by developing the growth share matrix, a tool that assesses a company's attractiveness within an industry. These frameworks are still used today by consultants to understand business problems and opportunities. They are also used in case interviews, business analysis questions commonly posed to prospective consultants. (More about cases later.)

Current Trends

Consultants and their clients are in a state of constant change. The typical client now requires more sophistication from its consultants' in-house skills and is more demanding in its requirements. For example, some clients now possess in-house strategy groups and have clear ideas of what their business means and the direction in which to head. Other clients demand more industry and content knowledge than the typical "generalist" strategist has. This increased requirement for sophistication means a number of new developments in the industry, which in turn will impact your decision to enter the industry.

Specialization

Insiders agree that the future of consulting seems to lie in the "boutique" (i.e., specialist) consulting firm. Boutiques have as few as two or three employees and as many as 150 or so, and they offer their clients highly specialized expertise, for example consulting solely to the biotech industry or providing expertise in marketing. Some of these firms were created by laid-off consultants or by those affected by recent mergers; others were founded by ex-partners of larger firms who wanted to strike out on their own with a specific area of expertise. These firms are often, by definition, much smaller than many generalist firms, but they are experiencing disproportionate growth, as clients increasingly demand depth, rather than breadth, from their strategic advisors. Successful boutiques are usually industry-focused (although sometimes they may be methodology-focused, or specialize in a single business function like operations or marketing), and could offer you the perfect job if you know what specific type of strategy work you are interested in.

The conventional wisdom at firms like McKinsey and Bain used to be to develop generalist consultants who could work across all sorts of industries, business functions and geographies. However, nowadays, clients increasingly demand that consultants come in with prior knowledge in some relevant area. While most of the larger firms still hire generalists, they ask consultants to specialize early in their careers, often only two or three years after starting at the company. So, as a newly-hired consultant at a generalist firm, you will work for a time on a wide variety of project types. But, after a couple years, you will be asked to focus on a particular area, and you will be increasingly placed on projects in just one industry or business function. Generalist firms sometimes also hire documented industry experts who might follow different (and possibly accelerated) career tracks than the standard-hire consultants. The so-called "rise of the super-boutique" involves not only rapid growth among specialist consulting firms, but the creation of highly specialized practices within the large formerly-generalist firms.

Project team structure

Another recent trend has to do with the structure of project teams. Large firms like McKinsey still leverage ample junior staff on projects, with both the firm itself and the project team reflecting a "pyramid" shape. This is not so at more and more firms. Diamond Management Technology Consultants (formerly DiamondCluster, which was formerly Diamond Technology Partners) talks not about the pyramid shape of the team but the "diamond" shape. On a large project at many consulting firms, you will have one to two partners, one to two analysts and/or junior consultants, and a bulge in the middle reflecting two to four more experienced consultants and project leaders. Why? Because clients have increased their demand for industry expertise and seasoned consulting chops—something that green BA and MBA grads lack.

Implementation planning

Many clients no longer want to pay for mere strategic musing. Hence, many strategic consulting firms now stay on to ensure implementation of their recommendations. That is, clients want the strategic recommendation to contain an implementation plan—a roadmap to put the strategy into play—and they often want the consultants to be available for the implementation, at the very least by phone and more often on a part-time basis at the client site.

Victims of the economy

The health of the consulting business is tightly tied to economic cycles. Be warned that as goes the economy, so goes the bounty of secure consulting jobs and interesting project work.

Consultants like to estimate future revenue for other industries. Speculation also abounds about revenue projections for the consulting industry itself. In the late 1990s, aggressive penetration of "emerging markets" (i.e., Asia, Eastern Europe, Latin America) by U.S. and multinational corporations, and rapid changes in client industries (privatization, IT changes and globalization) helped drive growth in the management consulting business.

All through the 1990s, consulting firms extended many offers and competed amongst themselves for the best candidates. It was a "seller's market" for talented BA and MBA graduates looking at consulting careers.

However, in the economic downturn of 2001-2003, consulting firms drastically scaled back hiring. The climate shifted abruptly and dramatically to a "buyer's market," where consulting firms extended few offers and shunned highly qualified candidates because they just didn't have enough open spots. Some firms stopped recruiting on campus for cost reasons, and resorted to delaying or rescinding job offers they'd made. Other consulting firms laid off consultants or sent them on unpaid or partially-paid "sabbaticals," to bring costs down to match reduced revenue. Internally, performance reviews became more frequent and a lot harsher; in fact, many former consultants feel like they were unfairly "counseled out" of their positions through an "up-or-out" review process.

For those consultants who survived such cuts, the mix of projects changed significantly. Potential clients turned away from strategic thinking to focus on costs, including process and operations redesign and downsizing. Companies were spending less on consulting budgets, so projects were smaller and the competition among consulting firms to get projects was fierce. In addition, there were fewer "pure strategy" projects in the overall consulting market. This was because, among consulting projects, strategy projects were considered a luxury, unless a company really needed to turn things around.

As a result, most strategy consultancies shifted their core competences to include operational work. Corporate clients turned to consultants as cheap labor, and even the largest and most prestigious consulting firms found themselves low-balling bids on tiny projects just to bring in some revenue.

2003 was the low point of this trend, but starting in 2004 things started picking up again as the economy rebounded. Today, consulting offers are once again relatively abundant, secure and financially lucrative; interesting strategy projects are on the radar once again as well.

This is all to say that while the consulting industry has so many merits, it is extremely risky. You may make a hefty six-figure salary as an MBA-level consultant, but you are very likely to experience a couple painful and costly years of unemployment during a long consulting career. And, once ejected from your consulting role (no matter what the reason you left), it is extremely hard to reenter the industry. As a general rule, consulting firms rarely seek or accept "lateral hires," or new consultants at any level other than first year post-BA and first year post-MBA. In fact, most of the consultant victims of the 2001-2003 economy never went back into consulting—timing alone meant that those graduates couldn't pursue the consulting career they had trained for and begun working in. Compare this risk profile to that of your doctor and lawyer classmates!

Despite the ups and downs, it's safe to say that consulting will never disappear—it will simply shift in emphasis. In the 1980s, business process reengineering was all the rage. Growth projects in strategy and IT kicked off the 1990s, and the e-business boom hit in the late 1990s. Turnaround was a major consulting trend of the early 2000s (when distressed clients need advice from consultants to cope with their economic situation). Today, consulting firms are scrambling to develop deeper expertise and market themselves as industry and methodology specialists to their clients.

And then there were four

Over the 1990s, the then "Big Five" accounting firms (Ernst & Young, KPMG, Arthur Andersen, PricewaterhouseCoopers, Deloitte) saw their management consulting business revenue grow to rival audit revenue. This drove increased SEC scrutiny into potential conflicts of interest, prompting the firms to make plans to separate out their consulting divisions.

Ernst & Young started the trend with the sale of its consulting unit to Capgemini in 2000. Then, KPMG Consulting was spun off from KPMG in a 2001 IPO, creating BearingPoint. After the Enron scandal broke in 2001, Arthur Andersen ceased operations (though the firm was never convicted of wrongdoing). BearingPoint hired the majority of Arthur Andersen's business consulting employees (rather than acquire the firm itself with its then-ongoing legal issues). In 2002, PricewaterhouseCoopers announced an IPO of its consulting division, to be rebranded as "Monday," but then sold it off to IBM instead (being part of what would be eventually called IBM Global Services). That same year, Deloitte considered splitting off its consulting practice and rebranding it as "Braxton," but ultimately decided to remain an integrated services firm, with management consulting and audit/accounting under one roof. Today, we have the "Big Four" audit firms of Ernst & Young, KPMG, PricewaterhouseCoopers and Deloitte—with Deloitte being the only one with a management consulting practice. Capgemini, BearingPoint and IBM are now major management consulting players worldwide.

Up, up and away

"Up-or-out" refers to the practice of requiring employees to either advance their careers to the next level of responsibility or move out of the firm. Staying at the same level for a long time, no matter how well an employee performs at that level, is not an option like it is in corporate jobs.

Consultants are informed whether they are up to firm standards when getting performance reviews. In the standard model, employees are warned that if they don't improve their performance by a certain date, they will be asked to resign from the firm. An employee and his or her manager agree upon a set of benchmarks by which they will measure performance improvements. The employee is usually not fired outright, but instead pressured to leave voluntarily. Depending on the particular firm's culture, these performance benchmarks may be concrete and clear, or evaluations may be more of a vague personality-based black box; the firm may provide an exiting employee with outplacement assistance, or might leave him high and dry with no severance and no unemployment payments (neither of which apply unless an employee is fired).

Firm loyalists defend the up-or-out approach as simply meritocracy at work, while others astutely point out that who stays and who goes is often quite political and relationship-based. Nonetheless, consulting firms must somehow reduce the size of each "class" of consultants as it moves up the hierarchy, in order to maintain the "pyramid" structure that enables their profitability. Faster-growing firms don't need to thin their numbers quite as much (because their whole pyramid can afford to get wider), and are therefore better bets for advancing all the way up.

In the economic downturn of 2001-2003, many firms turned to "counseling out" employees at all levels, putting them through a difficult series of review cycles with short time frames (in some cases as short as three to six months). This accelerated review process has been used by firms as a way to effect layoffs without actually firing employees (and subsequently incurring the costs of firing). According to many consultants, this highly competitive climate persists, even as the economic situation has improved. New recruits, especially those with a graduate degree, therefore face significant pressure to get on the right projects where they can quickly and effectively prove their worth.

How clients pay consulting firms

Consulting contracts take two basic forms: fixed price and time and materials. Most contracts are some form of fixed price, where the consulting firm might specify something like "$500,000 for a 10-week engagement" or "a run rate of $50,000 per week for 10 weeks." This bid price is calculated by the consulting firm by assuming a daily billing rate for each consultant on the proposed project team, figuring out what percentage of each week the consultants will be involved in the project, and adding it all up for the expected duration of the project. This method of payment contrasts with time and materials, where the contract specifies an hourly rate for each consultant and the client bill is paid out based on hours tracked by the consultant. Time and materials is the law firm model, and is prevalent in economics and litigation consulting firms, but not for most other management consulting firms.

In both cases, expenses for food, travel and administrative needs are separate from professional fees. Typically, expenses for a project can run 10 to 20 percent of the professional fees, and even higher for international engagements where the flights are more expensive and the hotel stays are longer. Guidelines for expense expectations are usually built into the engagement contract.

Pay for performance

Less frequently (but also worth noting), some clients use their buying power to insist that consulting firms accept pay-for-performance plans, termed "sweat equity" or "revenue sharing." A change from the billing typical among consulting firms, this form of payment gained some steam in the late 1990s when sweat equity was a popular means of compensating the thousands of dot-com employees who traded long, hard hours for shares in a company without revenue—some buyers of consulting services also found this to be a compelling payment model. Occasionally, you will see consulting firms boast about their use of revenue sharing as a means of putting their money where their Microsoft apps are. In principle, it's admirable to have consulting fees on the line as a means of proving your intent to do the best work you can. But it's not that common a payment structure, likely because it's a complicated one. It's simpler to hire a consultant for an engagement for a clear duration and price, rather than allow them to share in a huge upside if business goes as well as expected.

Business process outsourcing (BPO)

The number of clients willing to pay for elaborate strategic projects waxes and wanes—but management consulting firms need to keep revenue high. Publicly-traded firms like IBM also need to show consistent revenue growth, lest their stock price suffer. One specialty that offers the possibility of this revenue growth is business process outsourcing (BPO). (Note that BPO is not considered to be management consulting, but rather a type of operations and technology consulting that is tactical and technical in nature. Nonetheless, some management consulting firms have BPO as a service offering.)

BPO is the practice of outsourcing a non-core capability—for example, human resources services, call centers, billing departments, treasury services or training employees in Access. For example, General Motors outsources its travel expenses and corporate card charges—massive in a 100,000 person company—to a travel specialist. One of the largest outsourced capabilities? Printing. In 2001, printing services represented a $150 billion dollar market, according to *CFO Magazine*. Since most companies don't want to run their own printing plants, they hire a consultant to help outsource their non-core services. Consulting firms determine what needs to be outsourced in a company, locate the appropriate providers (sometimes themselves) and manage the process for clients. Accenture is an example of a firm that in the last several years successfully launched a major business endeavor into outsourcing.

BPO is a growth field, but it's not a particularly profitable field. It's a service line that doesn't offer as much room for differentiation, meaning more competition for BPO clients and lower profits. Furthermore, consultants tend to find BPO assignments tedious. On the other hand, BPO business units provide stable, predictable revenue for the company, which is better for your job security if you're a core part of it.

Consulting Versus Other Career Paths

Consulting is just one of many desirable professional career paths. Especially if you are at the undergraduate level, you are probably considering three or four other professions at the same time, including continuing your education right away in graduate school. We touch on a couple of these briefly for some reference, but we strongly encourage you to research them to a much greater extent on your own.

Investment banking

A lot of undergraduates and MBAs ask the question: "consulting or banking?" There are similarities between the two careers—including the high compensation relative to corporate positions, long hours and client focus—but the two tracks are very different.

It is very difficult to describe investment banking in a paragraph or two, but we'll take a shot at it anyway. In short, investment banks help companies raise money. Companies need money (capital) to grow their businesses, and investment banks sell securities (stocks or bonds) to public investors in order to generate these funds. Investment banks might also help a company merge its assets with that of another company, manage and invest the money of wealthy individuals or institutions, or buy and sell securities to make money for itself.

One clear advantage of investment banking over consulting is pay. On average, new investment banking analysts make $10-20,000 in total compensation more than their consulting counterparts (total compensation means base salary plus a targeted, but not guaranteed, bonus). MBA-level investment bankers start off at a similar compensation level to MBA-level consultants, but the banker salary quickly skyrockets to a point where a first-year managing director at an investment banking firm makes around one-and-a-half times what a first-year consultant partner makes. (See the income comparison chart toward the end of this book for further information on income levels.) Another very attractive feature of investment banking is that the work is very high profile. Since all of the deals become public, the work your team does will make it in *The Wall Street Journal* and other publications. For example, if you work for Merrill Lynch and you help TechCo go public, you might read in the newspaper how Merrill Lynch was the "lead underwriter" for TechCo's IPO. Investment banking suits the deal-driven person, one who works off of adrenalin and gets a personal thrill out of chasing and closing a deal. Banking is more heavily quantitative on a regular basis than consulting, though quantitative skills are important for both fields.

The biggest disadvantage is that, on average, the hours in investment banking (especially at the junior levels) can be very long. How long? Try 100 hours a week as a realistic possibility. That means working 15 to 18 hours a day and frequent all-nighters. And hours are even less predictable than those of consulting. Deals close or change at a moment's notice. The work tends to be much less flexible for employees with special scheduling needs—parents, for example. On the bright side, investment banking careers usually involve far less travel than consulting positions (though sometimes you have to fly out at a day's notice when a dormant deal suddenly awakens).

Corporate jobs

Corporate positions (at big companies like Coca-Cola, Procter & Gamble or Kraft, or at smaller outfits like Dow Corning, Timberland or Lattice Semiconductor), are another option. Many of the largest corporations offer management training programs to undergraduates and MBAs, where the new employee spends three to six months in a certain business unit before moving onto another one. At the end of 18 to 24 months, the employee typically chooses a business unit and stays there.

Compared to management consulting, corporate business careers historically have offered better job security, less travel and shorter hours in exchange for less pay and more bureaucracy. Flexibility and diversity is pegged strongly to individual corporate culture—some cultures are terrific, others terrible. The work can be just as compelling as consulting, and while you might make less money, you'll be in your own bed nearly every night. In fact, if you find a smart, fast-paced corporate environment in which to work, your job profile will be very similar to that of a management consultant in a firm with an as-needed travel policy.

Corporate jobs are also fantastically more plentiful than consulting firm jobs. Just think: There are on the order of just a couple hundred thousand management consultants in the U.S., compared to the many, many millions of corporate businesspeople!

Graduate school

Some people suggest that working for a few years before returning to graduate school is a smart idea. This can make a lot of sense if you are considering medical or law school. If you're looking at MBA programs, you should definitely get some work experience prior to applying, as top MBA programs admit very few candidates each year who have not had four to five years of full-time work experience. While fewer people work before law school or medical school, it's still a smart idea—you'll gain business knowledge and perhaps save some money for the long, impoverished school days ahead.

You might also be considering entering a masters or PhD program, which is an entirely different route. If you are most interested in teaching and research in a certain field, then perhaps a PhD is the way to go. You will enjoy an environment that is intellectually exciting. It can be a long road to the degree and professorship, however, and there are no guarantees of a tenured position.

You should be aware that while MBAs and undergrads are most appealing to recruiters, most consulting firms will consider a variety of graduate degrees in their applicant pool. If you take the recruiting firm point of view, you could imagine hiring the following:

- An MD with business acumen to work specifically in a firm's life sciences practice

- A PhD in physics who can offer a structured problem-solving approach to complex strategy projects
- An JD who can jump right into assisting a litigation consulting firm

The reality is that your odds are against you—if you are truly focused on consulting, your best bet is to get in right out of your undergraduate program or a top MBA program. But don't give up hope if you have an MA in Slavic Studies. Just focus on acquiring some real-world business experience that you can speak to in the interview process.

One more thing: A non-business graduate school degree is usually considered lesser than an MBA in terms of starting level or salary. If you don't have a master's, you would likely start as a business analyst. With a PhD, MD or JD, you would be likely to start at the level between business analyst and first-year MBA. This makes sense for any number of reasons, the most important of which being that you aren't coming in with direct relevant business training. Don't sweat it too much—you'll be better positioned for success in this new career if you start at the prescribed level, as you won't be competing with hungry MBAs for the next promotion right off the bat.

Folks with non-MBA graduate degrees should look strongly at boutique consulting firms, which tend to hire from a wider variety of sources than do the big generalist consulting firms. This is true especially if you bring in a relevant skill to the table—for example, that MS in biotechnology might come in handy at a consulting firm focused on (you guessed it) biotechnology clients. (More on boutiques later.)

Consulting Categories

CHAPTER 2

Types of Consulting Services

The types of advisory services that management consulting firms offer fall into six primary categories: pure strategy, operations strategy, marketing strategy, information technology strategy, financial strategy and human resources strategy. (See the following exhibit for how these areas fit together.)

The business consulting landscape

Financial consulting
Marketing consulting
Management consulting
- Marketing strategy
- Financial strategy
- HR strategy
- Pure strategy
- Operations strategy
- Technology strategy

HR consulting
Operations consulting
Technology consulting

Management consulting firms address business problems in marketing, finance, HR, operations and technology in addition to general business strategy. Large management consulting firms usually touch on all of these types of strategic problems, though individual partners may specialize in one particular functional area. Boutiques may work on many types of strategic problems in a single industry vertical (e.g., health care, financial services), or apply themselves to one functional area across a variety of industries (e.g., marketing, operations), or even specialize in a single analytical methodology (e.g., real options, economic value added).

In order to understand this industry, it's important to be clear that there are vast areas of business consulting that are not considered to be part of the "management consulting" arena. For example, much of "technology consulting" consists of systems integration and programming work, which is not strategic in nature. (As a case in point, Accenture has some 100,000 technology consultants in its fold, but reports that only a few thousand of them are technology strategy consultants, a.k.a. management consultants.) Similarly, much of both operations and financial consulting falls outside of management consulting.

Generalist consulting firms take on projects in all six of these areas, while individual consultants within the firm tend to spend much of their time with just one type of strategic problem. In contrast, highly specialized firms known as "boutiques" might focus on just one of these six types of strategy problems (and/or focus on just one industry). Many of the largest firms also provide consulting services outside of the management consulting space, offering IT implementation, financial advisory services or business process outsourcing.

Historically, consulting firms made their recommendations and walked away. Increasingly, however, clients expect management consultant strategists to stick around and implement their suggestions. Consequently, more consulting firms now tout their implementation capabilities in all of the six sub-areas of management consulting. "Implementation" is a vague term that might involve extensive process reengineering, selecting a software package, or simply being on tap to answer follow-up questions as the company takes action on the strategic recommendations.

Strategy consulting

By definition, problems that management consulting firms deal with are all strategic in nature. But there is a special category of problems sometimes called "pure strategy," or simply shorthanded as "strategy." It can get confusing, because consultants working on marketing strategy, operations strategy, et al, also like to shorthand those projects as "strategy" projects.

A "pure strategy" consulting engagement aims to help a client's most senior executives (for instance, the CEO and board of directors) understand and face the macro-level challenges of running their company or organization.

Examples of typical strategy consulting engagements:

- Recommending a new strategic direction for a growing wireless company
- Evaluating investment opportunities in a variety of industry sectors to support growth aspirations of a multinational company
- Understanding why Broadway theaters keep losing money and how the theaters can reposition themselves to profit most from new markets
- Determining the value of a PC manufacturer on a stand-alone basis and suggesting possible acquirers to help divest itself of non-core businesses

The largest firms known for their focus on "pure strategy" problems include:

- Bain & Company
- The Boston Consulting Group
- McKinsey & Company
- Booz Allen Hamilton

Marketing consulting

Management consultants who focus on marketing problems are fond of saying that "the marketing strategy is the strategy." And they have a good point—once you consider the five Ps of marketing (product, place, price, promotion, people), what is left out as far as defining a company's overall strategy? Consequently, oftentimes marketing consulting projects are aptly referred to simply as strategy projects. On these projects, consultants work with the senior marketing or business development leadership to shape overall marketing plans or develop detailed approaches to launch a new product or optimize existing ones.

Accordingly, the firms that are known for their expertise in marketing strategy consulting tend to be the ones well-known for their expertise in strategy consulting problems. There are a small handful of boutique firms out there that do in fact focus on marketing problems, but not many. There are also companies out there that focus on more tactical problems like branding or advertising. These are not part of marketing strategy consulting as we define it.

Examples of typical marketing strategy consulting engagements:

- Positioning a snack manufacturer to enter China, determining types of snacks most wanted and assessing the market's willingness to pay for snacks
- Assessing which features of a medical device matter to which segments of physicians, and developing a target marketing plan with two differently-featured versions of the device
- Evaluating the return on investment in various marketing and sales activities
- Supporting the development of an annual marketing budget for the client's new service offering

Some firms well-regarded for their expertise on marketing strategy problems include:

- Monitor Group
- Copernicus Marketing Consulting
- Simon-Kucher & Partners

- Prophet

Operations consulting

Operations consultants examine a client's internal workings, such as production processes, distribution, order fulfillment and customer service. While a strategy project sets the firm's goals, an operations consulting project aims to ensure that clients reach these goals. Consultants doing operations strategy work might investigate customer service response times, cut operating or inventory backlog costs, or look into resource allocation. They improve distribution, heighten product quality, or restructure departments and organizations (a specialty of the reengineering craze of the early 1990s).

Operations consulting projects tend to last longer than many other types of management consulting engagements, lasting up to 12 months. By their nature, these projects are more likely to involve the consultant in an implementation phase as well.

Examples of typical operations consulting projects:

- Strategic sourcing for a manufacturing company (e.g., improving the efficiency of the company's relationships with suppliers)
- Streamlining the equipment purchasing process of a major manufacturer
- Determining how a restaurant chain can save on ingredient costs without changing its menu
- Working with a newly-merged commercial bank to increase its customer response efficiency
- Creating a new logistical database for a tire manufacturer
- Optimizing the size of a pharmaceutical sales force, given the recent entry of two new competitive drugs into the client's space

The largest firms known for their focus on operations strategy problems include:

- Accenture
- A.T. Kearney
- PRTM
- Kurt Salmon Associates

Information technology strategy consulting

Information technology strategy (or "IT" strategy) consultants help clients achieve their business goals by leveraging in-depth knowledge of computer and telecommunications hardware, software and the inner workings of the Internet. It's important to understand that in the world of IT, there are both IT strategy consultants and IT implementation consultants, and the latter far outnumber the former. IT strategy consultants focus on how to leverage technology solutions toward meeting their business strategy direction, while IT implementation consultants do the real work to execute that strategy. IT implementation consultants design technology processes, custom software or networking solutions, test for system and program compatibility, and ensure that the new system is properly implemented. IT strategy consultants (who fall under the umbrella of "management consulting") focus on which technology road to take, rather than how the client gets there.

IT strategy practices (which embody an enormous percentage of worldwide consulting revenue) can be found within large consulting firms that also do implementation (think Big Four). However, the IT strategy groups have different personnel, project mix and billing rates from their IT implementation counterparts. Slightly confusing is the organization of IT strategists into vertical or horizontal groupings. Take risk management, for example. In some firms, this is located in specific industry groups like financial services or energy that also deal with implementation. On the other hand, a firm might also have a focused IT strategy group that deals exclusively with tech strategy projects across all verticals. If you're into IT strategy, do some digging to determine which is the case for your target firms.

Some people think that IT strategy has a lower bar than pure business strategy for new hires and is therefore a back-door way to get into a major consulting firm; examples include the McKinsey Business Technology Office (BTO) and Booz Allen's IT strategy practice. Don't be fooled. McKinsey has a "same-bar" method of interviewing where McKinsey BTO applicants go through exactly the same case interview rounds that other McKinsey consultants go through. You'll still need to bone up on those case interviews, and you'll need to bring to bear technical know-how in addition to strategy framework expertise.

IT strategy sometimes blends with process, which embraces hot technology trends denoted by various acronyms. In particular, know the basics of ERP (enterprise resource planning), and CRM (customer relationship management) before you walk into an IT consulting interview.

Be warned that IT strategy projects last even longer than operations projects; such projects can last 18 to 24 months. If you really crave a variety of different engagements, IT consulting is probably not for you.

Examples of typical IT strategy consulting engagements:

- Evaluating the benefits and costs of establishing a new Internet-based B2B exchange that facilitates optimal sourcing for the automotive industry
- Recommending that a bank incorporate a Sarbanes-Oxley system to support its risk management department
- Determining how a major "big-box" retailer can leverage technology to improve its distribution network
- Analyzing the benefits of wireless technology for a global shipping company

The largest firms known for their focus on information technology strategy problems include:

- Accenture
- Deloitte Consulting LLP
- Diamond Management & Technology Consultants
- IBM Global Services
- McKinsey

Financial strategy consulting

Financial strategy is one more of the many types of problems for which a company can hire management consultants. Working on these problems—whether as a one-off staffing assignment in a generalist consulting firm, or as an employee of a specialty financial strategy consulting practice—can be particularly rewarding for quantitatively-focused individuals with skills in accounting or financial statement analysis.

There are three primary categories of financial strategy projects:

- *Corporate finance* projects involve assisting clients with capital budgeting, P&L reporting, and/or project valuation.
- *Risk management and insurance* engagements involve helping clients think about controlling their various risk exposures, as well as planning for disaster scenarios.
- *Corporate restructuring or "turnaround"* consulting gigs involve a holistic renovation of a company's strategy and operations, where the consultants often step in as temporary management through challenges such as Chapter 11 bankruptcy.

This last category of financial strategy projects deserves special note. Turnaround consulting firms are a rare and selective breed of advisory services firm that tends to attract a similar profile of employee as investment banks. The work is transactionally-focused, fast-paced, and headline-oriented. It's fair to think about turnaround work as an element of management consulting in that you are advising client firms at a very senior level—however, the decisions being made involve not only big-picture ones, but also the crucial tactical issues of layoffs, facility closures, and the nitty-gritty of cost-cutting.

Large management consulting firms like Deloitte may have a specialized sub-practice in finance, but there are very few standalone financial strategy consulting firms. That's because finance is a core part of any business, so large corporations tend to build up this sort of expertise in-house, rather than outsource it to a consultancy. In major companies, you will find substantial corporate departments such as "risk management" or "treasury" that have a full-time cadre of financial analysts. (Note that many large corporations may outsource back-office financial processing to an Accenture, IBM, or EDS—but that type of work is outsourcing, not consulting.)

Don't get confused by the management consulting firms and practices that do financial services consulting (e.g. Oliver Wyman, or a financial services partner within Bain). Those consultants are helping *financial companies* with *all types of strategic problems*. More than likely they are helping, say, a credit card issuer develop a target marketing scheme, or a commercial bank decide whether to exit the mortgage business. Working as a financial strategy consultant means that you are helping *all types of companies* with *financial strategy problems*. Sorting this out during your job search process is easily solved by repeatedly clarifying recruiters' sales pitches to you with two questions: "What industries are your client companies in?" and "What type of problems do you advise those companies on?"

Examples of organizations that offer financial strategy consulting services include:

- Alix Partners (corporate restructuring)
- Deloitte (enterprise risk management)
- Marsh (risk management and insurance)
- McKinsey
- Monitor
- Protiviti (risk management)

Human resources strategy consulting

The best business strategies, the most thoughtful marketing plans and the most streamlined operations mean nothing if no one can put them into place. That's why HR consulting as a specialization remains robust. Companies know that investing in human capital pays off. Human resources consultants maximize the value of employees while placing the right people with the right skills in the right roles. This kind of HR consulting, also known as organizational development or change management, is one of the hottest consulting fields. Clients hire HR consultancies as part of departmental or organizational restructuring, systems implementations, and ongoing initiatives and studies (e.g., diversity and work/life balance).

For the most part, HR consulting is performed by specialist HR consulting firms, a.k.a. "boutiques." Much of HR consulting is more tactical than strategic, and therefore isn't truly part of the management consulting world.

Examples of typical human resources strategy consulting engagements:

- Bringing together the cultures of merged companies by developing or altering work cultures
- "Managing relationships" to ensure focus on customers and open communication
- Fostering employee creativity through "process innovation"

Examples of human resources consulting engagements of a more tactical nature:

- Building "competencies" through better and more efficient training programs
- Counseling and processing laid-off employees and assisting them in finding new jobs
- Creating or updating a new division's benefits package
- Reviewing and revising a law firm's compensation structure

The largest firms known for their focus on human resources strategy problems include:

- Mercer
- Hewitt Associates
- Towers Perrin
- Watson Wyatt Worldwide

Types of Firms

We've outlined the six types of advisory services that consulting firms offer. Now let's understand in what kinds of organizations one can work on those problems. There are three types of firms in which one can work: generalist consulting firms, specialist or 'boutique' consulting firms, and internal corporate consulting divisions.

Generalist management consulting firms

We know and love these folks. They are usually the large firms, and consequently the well-known ones. They attempt to be everything to everybody, and by and large succeed at it. The mix of what types of problems each firm tackles can vary greatly, of course. For example, McKinsey does lots of pure strategy and some amount of IT strategy through its BTO offering. Accenture has less than 5 percent of its revenue coming from pure strategy, but has a tremendous technology offering that stretches beyond IT strategy into systems integration. When consulting trends change, these firms adjust their services as well—as we mentioned before, BCG took on more operational improvement projects than usual during the cost-cutting era of 2001-2003. But what differentiates these firms from others is that their marquee offering over time remains pure strategy.

Working at a generalist firm means that you will work on a dizzying variety of projects initially, though by the time you are a few years post-MBA, you'll be asked to align with one practice area and specialize in a given industry or problem type.

Examples of generalist management consulting firms include the following:

- Accenture
- Bain & Company
- The Boston Consulting Group
- Booz Allen Hamilton
- Dean & Company
- IBM Global Services
- McKinsey & Company
- Monitor Group
- Oliver Wyman
- The Parthenon Group
- Roland Berger Strategy Consultants

Specialization among management consulting firms

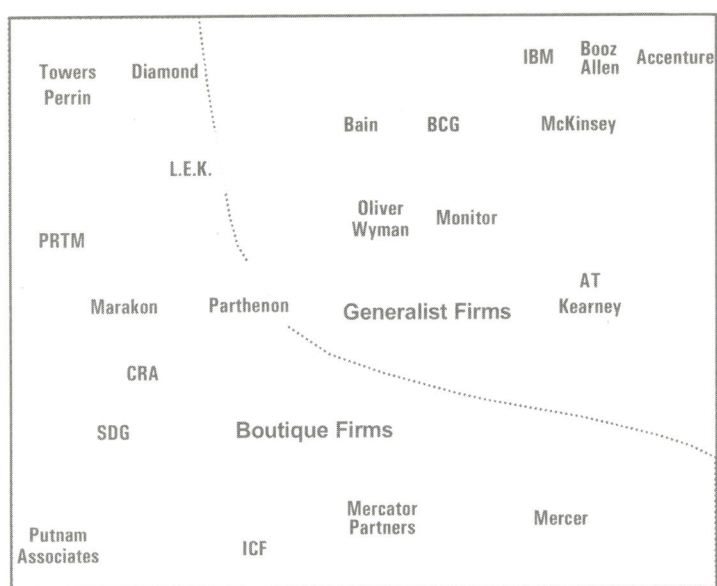

Degree of specialization by business function or methodology

Boutique (or specialist) management consulting firms

We're going to talk a fair amount about boutiques here for two reasons: (1) they still aren't understood very well and (2) they are an ever-increasingly important source of jobs at all levels.

Boutique firms support their clients with highly-specialized expertise. These firms choose to focus on a smaller number of industries (energy, life sciences, retail) and/or business problem types (marketing, operations, HR, technology, finance). Some offer targeted advisory services in a very narrowly-defined functional area (M&A, economics and litigation, turnaround) or methodologies (real options, EVA).

There are a couple common misconceptions about boutique firms. One is that being a "boutique consulting firm" necessarily implies being a small firm. This is not the case. A boutique is determined not by size, but by focus. L.E.K. Consulting (which was founded by a handful of former Bain partners) now has roughly 500 employees, but we would consider the company a boutique because of its specific focus on three types of strategy consulting problems: M&A, shareholder value and business strategy.

Another misconception is that boutiques are less prestigious than the multi-functional firms. This highly depends on the area of focus. For example, BCG is extremely well-regarded across many industries for most types of strategy problems, but for a decision analysis or real options strategy problem, clients would turn to Strategic Decisions Group, which has the best reputation in the business for these sorts of problems.

Because boutiques offer such depth in particular areas, it is increasingly common to find a boutique firm (and potentially a very small one with just a few employees) as the consultant of choice for a Fortune 500 company. These highly-regarded specialist firms are extremely appealing employers for prospective consultants who are interested in developing a true expertise, and who are not obsessed with working at a firm more well-known among the general public. (For a visual on where boutique firms fit into the consulting landscape, see the following exhibit.)

All this said, we should note that many boutiques are indeed small, ranging from upwards of 200 employees down to a single consultant. Often, boutique consulting firms grow from the expertise and client relationships of one to five founding partners, and unless it sells a consistently large flow of work, the firm has no compelling reason to grow quickly. Also, smaller boutiques can deliver services at lower costs than the larger consultancies because a smaller firm requires less overhead and less extra "capacity" (i.e., consultants), so their services might seem more attractive to prospective clients than those of the more expensive firms.

If you are especially interested in a particular industry or type of consulting problem, definitely do your homework on the outstanding boutiques in that field. They are hard to find, so use a combination of Google searches, news clippings, online directories and good ol' fashioned networking to locate boutiques that are more than a "fly-by-night" or "single-shingle" with a nifty web site. If you find the right company to match your interests (and you have the self-awareness to know what those core interests are), you will spend all of your consulting career doing the work you most enjoy—and trust us, that is a much harder goal to achieve within a generalist consulting firm.

Examples of possible consulting projects in a boutique firm:

- A consulting firm with a well-known shareholder value methodology helps a beverage company establish value metrics in its business units
- An economics consulting firm helps a foreign government decide how to structure the privatization (sale) of its utilities through an auction

I smell a fraud: calling out the weak boutiques

Boutiques can be great places to work ... but not all of them.

Here is a true story: A consulting firm founded several years ago by two state university BAs who met working at a lesser-known tech firm now wants to take on a third person. They've been surprisingly successful driving new business to date due to their talent for salesmanship, but now want to add some serious pedigree to improve their competitiveness for bigger-name client prospects. Their carefully-selected new hire can boast a Stanford University undergrad degree in engineering, work experience at Goldman Sachs and BCG, an MBA from HBS and quantitative analysis skills that the two founders just can't touch. The dynamic duo proceeds to leverage the new hire to the hilt:

- New project pitch documents make the new hire sound like multiple people: "We've got a team from Stanford and Harvard Business School, as well as folks from Goldman Sachs and BCG."

- Asked by a client about financial management experience, one of the founding partners pats the newly-hired consultant on the back as he touts their depth of experience, saying, "With this guy's experience at Goldman Sachs and all, we've on occasion parachuted him into struggling companies to serve at interim CFO." The new consultant, humiliated by the fabrications, can only nod weakly.

- Responsibility for the entire analytical portion of projects is dumped into the new hire's lap. The founders don't review or critique his Excel models, because they aren't familiar with the functions and programming features used. The "two heads are better than one" adage goes out the window, with the new consultant guiltily making it up as he goes along.

Time and again we've heard stories like this one, where a consultant (particularly one with a name-brand background that can be leveraged in marketing) believes she's discovered a great career opportunity with a tiny boutique firm. At this firm, she'll be given more responsibility much faster than will her peers at larger firms, plus she'll avoid the bureaucratic downsides of larger firms, while possibly getting paid somewhat better too. However, many times, this extremely intelligent and educated consultant finds herself surrounded by peers and supervisors who lack her same level of intellectual rigor, analytical capability, and sophistication in crucial "soft skills." The consultant doesn't feel that there's anyone around to learn from, and tension develops when the firm's leaders feel intimidated by the very talent that they purposefully sought to hire.

The lesson is once you've found a boutique consulting firm that interests you, you need to ask hard questions in order to understand that it has a robust business model, that the firm's leaders are people you can respect and learn from, and that the work you will be doing is appropriate for your experience and knowledge level.

Here is one common statement to watch out for: "We go up against McKinsey all the time when we're selling work, and often win." Many boutiques state this claim with evident giddiness, as if it validates their existence. But this is a ridiculous statement. Why?

- McKinsey is the largest management consulting firm in the world. It is involved in nearly every industry and type of strategic advisory project that you can imagine. So, a company had better be going up against McKinsey fairly often. Otherwise something's wrong!

- McKinsey can't win every single beauty pageant. First of all, it is too busy pitching work to too many potential clients; while a little boutique puts weeks of effort into pitching its heart out for a small, $100k project, McKinsey has bigger fish to fry and may throw a generic proposal written by a low-level consultant at that RFP without much attention. Secondly, McKinsey is one of the most high-priced consultancies out there, and often loses in competitive situations to the little boutiques that substantially underbid them. So any given consulting firm—especially that small gem of a boutique you discovered and interviewed with—had better be beating McKinsey some of the time. If not, something's wrong!

So call the bluff and ask some pointed questions: How long have you been in business? What is the background of the partners? What are their credentials as consultants? What was the average revenue generated per partner? How does the firm deal with project staffing? Does the firm use a lot of outside consultants or contractors? What are the firm's long-term goals for hiring? What are the firm's long-term goals in terms of positioning and business development? What is the company's competitive advantage over others in its class, including McKinsey?

> Boutiques are both hard to find and hard to investigate, and it is a slight risk to join one without an established brand name. But if you look hard enough, you can certainly find one that offers a uniquely fast-paced development opportunity, highly compelling work content and the entrepreneurial environmental that most of us crave.

- A niche R&D strategy consulting firm deploys two consultants to a high-growth semiconductor company in Silicon Valley for a three month project to improve R&D processes
- A process reengineering boutique snares a six-month project to assist implementation of new supplier standards for an automotive consortium
- A turnaround consulting firm helps a telecommunications hardware firm restructure its organization until Chapter 11 bankruptcy
- A market research specialty firm conducts a quantitative survey of 500 physicians, using the results to perform statistical analysis in SPSS and generate inputs for a probabilistic simulation model of pharmaceutical product demand

Some of the more well-known boutique consulting firms include:

- CRA International (economics and litigation consulting)
- ICF Consulting (energy)
- L.E.K. Consulting (shareholder value, M&A, and business strategy)
- Marakon Associates (shareholder value methodology)
- Mercator Partners (telecom strategy)
- Putnam Associates (life sciences)
- Strategic Decisions Group (strategy consulting using decision analysis)

Internal consulting divisions

Recognizing a constant need for third-party expertise, some corporations have established formalized internal consulting units. Consultants from these units report to a central consulting division, which then staffs its employees within different business units in the company for assistance on issues such as corporate strategy, business development and project management. The consultants remain deployed with the client for either a set period of time or throughout the duration of a specific project. Even though everyone technically works for the same company, the consulting arm acts as an outsider, since its consultants don't work for the business units.

Why don't these corporations hire outside consultancies? One reason why corporations like having internal consulting groups is cost savings. Internal consulting groups can be an economical way to obtain a large amount of consulting help. The firm doesn't have to pay the exorbitant billing rates; instead, it can receive the "outsider" opinion for a corporate pay scale. The firm also benefits from having a dedicated team of experts knowledgeable on the company and its industry. In addition, having a dedicated internal consulting unit is a smart way for corporations to market themselves and attract top talent from the outside consulting ranks.

You should think of internal consulting as the same role as if you were in a typical external consulting firm, except on permanent retainer for the same client. You are simply on the client side of the table, and your paycheck comes directly from the client. The main disadvantages to being an internal consultant instead of a "normal" consultant is that you don't get the same variety of industries as you would elsewhere, and you are probably paid at corporate salaries, which are typically lower than consultant salaries. On the other hand, you will no doubt travel far less (except in the rare situations where you are on a long-term assignment off-site from company headquarters). And because you are not trying to win repeat work as a consultancy, you will not have the same face time pressures that you might as a typical management consultant. Job security is higher if you are on the corporate side as well.

Compared with working at a professional services firm, working internally at a corporation can be a less stressful, less competitive situation. You are unlikely to find the same territorialism among partners (or even the notion of equity partners), scrutiny over billable hours and project margins, insane hours and up-or-out attitude. If you are concerned about some of the "cons" of management consulting that we've mentioned throughout this book, but are attracted to the types of problems consultants address, you might find an internal consulting arm to be a great fit for you. Note that such departments are not always called "internal consulting"—most large companies have individuals or small teams whose role is to temporarily problem-solve for and advise whichever business unit needs help. Companies with formal internal consulting divisions offer more structure, a clearer promotion path and a better guarantee of getting true management consulting types of work. Nonetheless, working in a "corporate strategy" or "strategic planning" group—or as a single individual strategic analyst unaffiliated with any one department—often effectively means you are an "internal consultant."

One beef we've heard about internal consulting positions: location. Most external consultancies are based in some sort of major metropolitan area like Chicago or Boston. Large corporations often have their headquarters many miles from the nearest significant city—think Sprint in Overland Park, Kansas (apologies to those of you reading this who live there). There are pros and cons to most every aspect of consulting—if you want a house in the suburbs, you might be really happy at a company that isn't based in a major city, with your commute being as little as 10 minutes in a car. For many folks (especially newly-minted MBAs with newly-minted families) this is indeed a great way to go.

Examples of internal consulting projects:

- The strategic planning group of a large commodity trading business deploys three consultants to help its futures brokerage arm come up with a marketing strategy
- An internal consulting group at a large petrochemicals corporation hires a change management specialist for long-term deployment on a project with the marketing distribution operating unit, to assist in a multiyear implementation of SAP system
- An MBA analyst who reports directly to the CEO of a power company spearheads the development of a new market price forecasting methodology, leveraging some staff off the trading floor
- A management sciences group in a commercial bank supports the bank's venture capital investments

Some formalized internal consulting practices that actively recruit new BAs and/or MBAs include:

- American Express Strategic Planning Group
- Cargill Strategy and Business Development
- Johnson & Johnson Decision Sciences Group
- J.P. Morgan Chase Internal Consulting Services
- Proctor & Gamble Strategic Planning Group

GETTING HIRED

Chapter 3: Targeting Consulting Firms

Chapter 4: The Hiring Process

Chapter 5: What to Expect in the Interview

Chapter 6: Post-Interview: Accepting, Negotiating, Declining

Targeting Consulting Firms

CHAPTER 3

By now you've decided to pursue a career in consulting. You've spoken to real-life consultants, had a heart-to-heart with your career services counselors and made peace with the potential for long hours and brutal travel in exchange for intriguing project work and financial rewards. Now it's time to get started and choose prospects for where you'd like to work.

Researching Companies, the Right Way

Landing a consulting job takes a lot of time and effort, and company research plays an important role in a candidate's preparation. Prior to the 1990s, information on companies was not very easy to find. Candidates relied on word-of-mouth insights, company literature or the occasional book. With the advent of the Internet, the process of researching a company changed dramatically. Candidates are now expected to read a company's web site, understand the company's makeup and be prepared to talk about it in interviews. Completing this step in your preparation can be the difference between a job offer and a rejection letter.

Company basics

With all the information on potential employers readily available, it's all too easy to overdose. Consulting firms do not expect you to be an expert; but they do want you to have a basic grasp of their firm's history, current practice areas and targeted industries, major office locations, recent news developments and what key factors distinguish them from their competition. The important aspects are genuine interest in the consulting industry as a whole, the problem-solving prowess to excel as a consultant and the personal skills to work well with both the client and your project team.

Be comfortable with the basics of each firm, but don't let your research become an end in itself. Overzealous candidates often make this mistake. They feel compelled to ask three-layered questions about revenue streams and utilization rates to show recruiters just how much they prepared for the first interview. Recruiters are not particularly impressed by this behavior. On the other hand, they have even less patience for candidates who exhibit no knowledge of the firm whatsoever.

Core competencies

Keep your research simple and focused. Go to a firm's web site and learn the basics, making sure to find out the firm's core competencies or the skill sets that it expects each new hire to have. You should read the firm's annual report if it is publicly traded. If you are still in school, look up the firm of your dreams on LexisNexis and look for recent articles on the firm. Search your alumni database for folks employed there and ask to pick their brains over coffee.

A firm's core competencies can have a big impact on its culture, so knowing them will help you decide if the work environment will be agreeable. Remember, company research is not just to help you do well in an interview; it also will help you decide if the firm is where you want to be.

How do they interview?

Aside from learning about a company through its web site, you could benefit from knowing how the firm interviews. Do they ask case questions? Are there multiple interview rounds? Does the firm use interview panels, or is each interview conducted in a one-on-one format? Getting this information before the interview can lower your stress level and make you a more relaxed candidate. The best source is people you may know at the firm or friends who have gone through the interview process already. You can even address these questions to company recruiters. Armed with this information, your focus on the day of the interview will be much sharper, and your discussions will cover the topics that matter the most. (For insider information on the hiring process at top consulting firms, see the *Vault Guide to the Top 50 Consulting Firms* and Vault's consulting firm employer profiles.)

A little goes a long way

Once you've done all the necessary research on a firm, store it away in your memory for the actual interview. Use it in a very limited fashion, or mix it into discussions about your work experience, your personality and your goals. Think of your newfound company knowledge as a fail-safe cushion for questions such as "Why do you want to work here?", "What is it about our firm that interests you?" and "Why are you a good fit for our firm?" A little company information goes a long way with these questions. Leave your doctoral thesis at home, and do not be afraid to express your ignorance on certain topics. Recruiters appreciate a certain level of intellectual humility.

Understanding the different firms

Your mission: Find a firm that fits with your current goals and lifestyle and provides you with the experience you need for your next career move.

The truth is, very few of us will be lucky enough to have multiple job offers and have to make a job decision based on such specific criteria as the firm's travel model. Use the information you gather to eliminate firms you definitely wouldn't work at. But we encourage you to not be overly picky in your search. Keep an open mind—a firm you aren't in love with might wind up your only job offer. While you generally shouldn't apply to firms you wouldn't want to work at in reality (a similar rule of thumb applies when choosing potential undergraduate or graduate programs), you should also be practical about how competitive it is to make it into consulting in the first place.

Here is a short list of questions to help you understand the firms a little better. You might ask the following questions at the time of an interview or during your research phase.

What kind of consulting projects does the firm typically encounter?

Are you interested in working on high-level strategy issues, or do you prefer to roll your sleeves up and dig into the operational details of a company? How important is for you to be involved in the actual implementation of the strategy? Would you prefer to spend all of your time in one industry? See how employers fit with your preferences. Understanding yourself and your potential employers yields vital information about firms' working style and culture—and your suitability there.

Do analysts/associates work on more than one project (also known as an "engagement," or "case") simultaneously?

Some companies, like McKinsey and Booz Allen Hamilton, assign their associates and analysts to a single project at any given time. Others, like Bain or BCG, may staff consultants on two engagements at once. This results in a number of differences in working style.

- When on a number of studies at once, you often cannot get everything done in the time available. Therefore, you must become adept at managing expectations and delineating complex priorities and trade-offs. You also

- need to deal with the challenges of having multiple managers at once, both of whom compete for your time.

- If you plan on consulting for just a couple of years, consider your goals for breadth and depth of exposure to industries and study types. Judge if you prefer to dig into fewer areas in greater detail or to get maximum exposure to a wide range of experiences.

- Working on multiple projects normally means that you spend more time in the office than at the client's—after all, sitting at Client A's office discussing Client B's distribution problems on the telephone would be unprofessional. Be aware, however, that two or more clients means more opportunities for emergencies and hastily-called meetings that require your presence.

- Single projects generally last from a few weeks up to a year (or longer on some occasions). By the end of the project, depending on staffing needs, you might find yourself unwillingly pigeonholed into what has effectively became a new area of expertise.

- On the other hand, if you are on a single project, you generally have to travel to only one location for the duration of the project, and you might even be fortunate enough to know how long and for which days of the week you'll be there.

Do project teams include both consultants and active client representatives?

While almost all consulting firms mention "considerable client contact" as one of their attributes, examine this further. Discern if this means weekly meetings with senior client managers or daily interaction with client staff who provide full-time support to the project. Again, the answer to your query indicates a lot about the style of your projected work patterns:

- The typical model is to have a consulting project team that does the heavy lifting and reports to a client project team periodically. The consulting project team will also have interviews or data gathering meetings with various employees of the client firm. But for the most part, the consultants are off in their own "war room" huddled in front of scrawly flip charts with leftover Chinese food strewn on a desk.

- It's less common for consultants to pair up with clients to do the work together, but it happens. Sometimes working collaboratively with client team members can be challenging. They might need you to spend time explaining your consulting methodologies, and likewise you could find yourself struggling to pick up their company-specific jargon. Also, you might have to adjust your schedule to their other commitments and often disregard a reciprocal request.

- On the other hand, working with client team members can be the most valuable way for a consultant to spend his or her time. For one thing, you start to develop management skills (something many consultants lack). You also gain better insight into your client's industry and company (which is especially valuable if you ever want to consider jumping ship to a client at some point).

What is the travel model?

Some consultants enjoy extensive travel (and the accompanying frequent flyer miles), while others loathe the prospect of getting stuck at yet another airport lounge. Whichever type you are, learn about the firm's travel model. Firms like Accenture, Booz Allen Hamilton and McKinsey typically keep their consultants on client site four days a week, with Fridays in the office. Bain and BCG, on average, spend a lot of time on client site at the beginning and end of the project, but somewhat less in between. IBM Global Services makes no secret of its travel intensity, sometimes requiring of its consultants 100 percent weekly travel for several months. While every project has different travel needs, firms do have standard travel policies.

Also find out what proportion of engagements tend to be out of town. Nearly all of the large consulting firms work from offices in most major locations around the world. More localized competitors like Monitor or Parthenon usually send their consultants to faraway destinations for extended periods because they normally don't have a physical presence near the client.

Does the consulting firm have offices worldwide, or is it based in a small number of key cities? How does this compare with its client distribution?

Ask about the firm's policy on staffing between offices. Some consultancies take a more pan-regional approach to staffing projects, especially in European and Asian offices. This means that even if you work in the London office, you might find yourself shipped off to Hungary or Chiang Mai. Consulting firms with strong specializations are also more prone to send consultants on extended trips—specialized assignments require the best consultants, no matter where they might be based.

Also ask about how each firm distributes its offices: geographically or by specialty. While most firms today organize their offices geographically, some still retain what are commonly called "centers of excellence" (or COEs). If you work for a COE, you will probably report geographically to that office, meaning you will most likely maintain your residence nearby. Some firms, like Diamond, allow consultants to live anywhere and work out of any of their offices, though they still must report administratively to the COE. Keep in mind that where you live impacts how far you travel and how long you stay away from home.

At what level do consultants begin to specialize by industry, function or geographic expertise?

Most people go into consulting without a clear sense of the industry or type of problem they would like to work on. However, especially with the continuing trend for clients to demand industry expertise, one can't stay general forever. The longer you stay in consulting, the more you will find yourself needing to specialize in both industry and type of problem in order to sell work and serve your clients well.

As you enter consulting, you might have a clear idea of an industry or functional area in which you wish to specialize. On the other hand, you might want to use consulting to remain industry-neutral in the short term, while assessing your options. Almost every firm encourages its consultants to choose an area of expertise as they increase in tenure; the question is, how quickly?

Undergrad hires usually stay generalist for their three to four years in the business analysis role. The track for MBA-level hires is a little different. In order to grant their new associate hires as much exposure as possible to different industries and types of problems, most large strategy firms prefer that their new hires follow a generalist track for a few years before specializing. But the MBA-level hires are requested to specialize so they can really nail the projects they deliver and eventually know an area well enough to sell it. That said, once you complete a few successful projects in a particular area, you are often asked to do others in that area, so try and manage your early project flow.

Specialization can be somewhat linked to training at a firm. All firms encourage training (at least in theory), some of which is general to the firm's methodologies, team leadership training or strategic selling. Other training modules are going to be specific to your area of specialty, which is not a bad thing if you like your area of specialization. Make sure you have a clear sense of when specialization kicks in because, as you can tell, it's slightly different everywhere and it can be impacted by your training modules and vice versa.

What else?

To complete your picture of the firm, you may want to find out a few other details. These include (but aren't limited to): turnover rate, vacation policy, unpaid leave policy, telecommuting options, feedback system and social atmosphere. Again, think about what is particularly important to you, and ask away. You may want to wait until you receive an offer to get into every last detail, however; otherwise, you'll look as if you're only concerned with the vacation policy or happy hours.

What isn't important at this stage?

Salary. You are probably wondering late at night how much money you're going to get paid. The salary question isn't actually off limit at this point, but you don't want to become distracted by this question.

The reality is that consulting firms constantly benchmark salaries against one another, and offer very similar pay packages to new hires. Occasionally, you'll find one firm that offers somewhat less because they are popular and can get away with it, or another firm that offers notably more because they are growing fast and desperate, or in need of specific expertise. You are definitely better off picking the right firm culture than choosing a firm that pays $3,000 a year more than another. Furthermore, the firm that offers a few thousand less initially might very well pay larger bonuses more often, have more generous raises or push consultants up the promotion path more quickly. Once you have the big issues out of the way in understanding differences among potential employers, you can look more closely at the tactical aspects of your compensation. It's otherwise very easy to get hung up on this one number at the expense of finding a good fit where you are most likely to succeed.

Some consultants tempt themselves into thinking that *revenue per consultant*, a metric published by most firms, tells them something about how much money they are going to get paid. It doesn't. This is a weird number that is calculated differently at every firm (in fact, it is the opinion of the authors of this guide that this metric is completely

> useless). If revenue per consultant is higher at one firm than the others, it means either that:
>
> (1) Billing rates are higher than at other firms, and the number of consultants is the same, or
>
> (2) Billing rates are equal to or lower than other firms, and the number of consultants is lower
>
> Good luck working there if (2) is the case, because projects are probably chronically understaffed and you'll be burning the midnight oil more often than not. If (1) is the case, then the firm likely has a pyramid structure where the billing is weighted toward the very top end of the pyramid (partners), and it's the partners that are making all the money, not you. Either way, who cares?
>
> We want to stress the point that you should focus on the more important things like the type of work you'll actually be doing, rather than minor gradations in compensation that in the long run won't make or break your household's wealth accumulation.

Interviewing the Consultants

Talking to current consultants at the firm of your choice is the best way to get the crucial information you want.

Think about the way you ask questions. For example, it is difficult to answer questions like "What's a typical day?" or "What are the projects like?" The answers might be vague, or perhaps the interviewer might tell you about the best three projects she worked on out of 20, which is not the answer you're looking for. Instead of asking to describe a few projects, ask for the last three. Instead of asking how many hours he or she typically works, ask how many hours he or she worked over the past two weeks. Instead of asking about a typical day, ask what they did yesterday and what they will do tomorrow.

You can take things a step further, however, and ask scenario questions. These can be fun to ask and can give you more truthful answers, especially when it comes to lifestyle-related questions. Here are some examples. If you're nervy enough, you can even ask your interviewer one or two of these!

• If you have a spare evening from work, how would you spend it?

- With your work schedule, could you commit to a Monday evening class at 6 p.m. at the local university? Or Thursday season tickets to the symphony?
- When did you come into work yesterday? When did you leave?
- When you and your colleagues go out for dinner or drinks, where do you go?
- How many Sundays did you work this year?
- How many times will you check your voice mail tonight?
- What business applications, such as Word, Excel, or @RISK, have you used for your reports? Your client presentations? Your financial models?
- Have you ever had to cancel dinner with your spouse at the last minute because of work?
- If you were CEO of your firm, what would you change about it?

You get the idea. Think about what's really important to you, and find a vivid, concrete way to ask it.

Most people are able to find current consultants to speak with at their target firms. We offer the following idea: Talk to former employees of the firm. They will have different (and occasionally more candid) opinions on the firm than will current employees.

There are two categories of former employees you should consider talking with:

- *Former employees who are still in consulting.* Why did the consultant leave? What did she like about the firm? What did she dislike? What does she find more appealing about her current firm? Would she work for the firm again, given the opportunity?

- *Former employees who are no longer in consulting.* Why did the person leave the consulting industry altogether? Was it this specific firm that turned her off to the industry as a whole, or was it simply the industry? What does she find about her current career more compelling than a consulting career, and what does she like better about the firm versus her current place of employment?

Get the BUZZ on Top Schools

Read what **STUDENTS** and **ALUMNI** have to say about:

- Admissions
- Academics
- Career Opportunities
- Quality of Life
- Social Life

Surveys on thousands of top programs
College • MBA • Law School • Grad School

VAULT
> the most trusted name in career information™

Go to www.vault.com

The Hiring Process

CHAPTER 4

The Recruiting Process: An Overview

The most valuable asset of any consulting firm is its human capital. Before clients see presentations, reports or results, they see consultants. Before clients work with products or services, they work with people. Consequently, consulting firms purposefully make their interviews intense and lengthy to measure your intellectual, physical and emotional stamina.

For a long time, consulting firms focused on recruiting a relatively small number of undergraduate and graduate institutions. When the dot-com boom occurred in the late 1990s, Internet startups that offered leadership positions and the smell of an early retirement stole many highly-qualified students away from the consulting firms. Realizing they might be missing out on talent elsewhere, consulting firms began to take a more open-minded approach to recruiting, including considering candidates with nontraditional advanced degrees, such as MDs or PhDs. This trend has continued and flourished, especially given the proliferation of boutique consulting firms that must look broadly for consulting talent.

A framework for getting the dream consulting job

Of course, it's possible to get on the radar screen if you come from a less traditional background or a college outside traditional recruiting haunts. While the competition for consulting jobs is extremely tough (even for initial interviews), there are ways you can increase your chances of being selected for an interview.

Keep in mind that there are many steps to take in order to get to the interview process. It is competitive just to get an on-campus interview; when firms choose not to come to your campus, or if you are trying to break in from another industry without contacts, the competition is much stiffer. Here's how to get those precious interviews.

For each firm in which you are interested, you will want to

(1) Tailor your resume and experiences to consulting.

(2) Find the appropriate contact, either through on-campus recruiting or networking. (You can ask an alum to point you to the right contact, for example.)

(3) Apply to the firm by crafting a cover letter specific to the firm, delivering it to the firm and following up by e-mail or phone.

(4) Arrive at the interview prepared and appropriately dressed.

We'll now talk about each of these areas in depth.

Tailoring Your Resume for Consulting

Consulting firms receive thousands of applications each year, both during recruiting season and otherwise. Your resume serves as an important tool for recruiters in the selection/elimination process. You increase your selection chances by tailoring your resume and cover letter to specific consulting firms and positions. Consulting recruiters look for the following on resumes:

- Evidence of academic strength. Some firms insist on this information and even set GPA/board score cutoff points. Scores are usually more important for undergraduates than MBAs or career changers.

- Team player characteristics. Consulting firms structure their teams very carefully. Some of them use complicated matrices to determine the best fit for each project based on available resources, necessary skills and training plans. Recruiters want people who can play their roles with flexibility and grace.

- Propensity for leadership and confidence. Consulting firms want employees with a senior management potential. They see all hires as either future partners or future clients. Consulting firms want to work with employees who already demonstrate a predisposition to leadership, not someone who needs to be taught from scratch. Evidence of such potential includes leadership positions held in college and/or the undertaking of new initiatives without support.

- Accomplishments. Firms seek people who boast long lists of accomplishments that demonstrate reliability, tenacity, commitment, motivation and high standards of excellence. Clients want to hire consultants who can get things done well, in a short amount of time and without too much hassle.

- Distinctions. You've got lots of competition. However, if you can differentiate yourself on your resume—highlighting technical skills, foreign languages, publications, awards, notable public appearances—it will be to your advantage.

- Client skills. Consulting is a client business. Consultants must work well with clients. Evidence of this might include a service-oriented job, like a part-time technical support position or a community service position.

In some cases, recruiters look for relevant functional expertise (e.g., engineering or finance) or for specific industry experience or technical skills. If you know this ahead of time, emphasize any germane experiences you have. Wherever possible, quantify your results to make your achievements more concrete and tangible.

Be aware that how you write and structure your resume says a lot about how you communicate with others. Make your resume as terse as possible, and make your layout easy on the eyes. A consultant's time is worth many hundreds of dollars per hour, and your client's time is equally important. No one involved has enough patience to read through copious paragraphs, so learn to use bullet points and get to the bottom line.

How to Strengthen a Non-Business Resume

It is true that consulting firms love to hire candidates with direct experience in business. Many don't have it. The good news is that you can strengthen your resume significantly by reframing your experiences in consultant language.

Keep in mind how consultants think: They assess the situation, define the problem, identify the solution and execute. They also look for management potential, leadership qualities and soft skills. You wouldn't be interested in consulting if you hadn't had similar experiences in your life, would you? For example, how did you research and identify your history thesis topic? You had to invent a methodology and answer an interesting question. Are you a doctor? Then every day you use situation assessments and hypotheses. Did you tutor a student part-time in calculus? Then you will likely be a solid people manager.

The following is an excerpt from a resume of an MBA student. Prior to business school, he worked for a fictitious investment bank called Smart

Brothers as a computer programmer. He is knowledgeable in C++ and Oracle and spent 80 hours a week in front of a monitor coding financial software engines and Windows applications. His challenge was to reflect skills that would interest a consulting firm. Here is how he wrote up his work experience:

SMART BROTHERS New York, NY

Project Manager—Information Technology June 2001—July 2005

- Managed project teams to develop profit and loss systems for Proprietary Trading group

- Promoted to project leadership role in two years, well ahead of department average of four

- Developed an original mathematical algorithm for trading processing module, improving performance by 1200%

- Led team of six analysts in firmwide project to reengineer loan syndicate trading flows in firm's largest technology project of 2005. Recommendations established new firmwide standard for real-time trade processing

- Appointed lead developer of interest accrual team after just three months in department. Initiated and designed project to create customized, improved interest accrual and P&L applications for fixed income controllers

- Selected to work on high-profile project to reengineer corporate bond trading P&L system. Reduced overnight processing time from six hours to 20 minutes and improved desktop application speed by 350%

- Devoted 20-25 hours a month instructing junior members of the team on interest accrual and trading

---

Note that this person doesn't speak to the content of his work as much as the process. We have no idea what kinds of software he really built or what computer languages he knows. On the other hand, we know that he managed teams, was dedicated enough to his job to achieve a fast promotion and was committed to building the knowledge base of his team. He also worked closely with his client base of users in order to solve their problems. In addition, he wrote a very results-focused set of bullet points, for example quantifying the performance improvements or mentioning how he established a new standard. This resume suggests not programmer, but consultant.

The moral of the story is to think carefully about your past experiences and reframe them as if they were consulting projects; you will be pleasantly surprised and recruiters will be impressed.

Sample Resumes and Cover Letters

On the following pages, we've compiled some examples of consulting resumes and cover letters that have found success in the job market. These job search materials have been compiled by Vault editors from currently employed consultants at top firms.

EUGENE H. HUANG
5050 S. Lake Shore Dr., Apt. 1407
Chicago, IL 60615
(773) 555-1234
ehuang@uchicago.edu

EDUCATION

MIDWAY SCHOOL OF BUSINESS — Chicago, IL
Master of Business Administration – Finance and Strategic Management — June 2007
- Dean's Honor List
- Active member of Management Consulting, Corporate Management and Strategy, and High Tech Clubs.

ANDERSEN COLLEGE — Boston, MA
Bachelor of Arts in Physics (Cum Laude) — June 2002
- Andersen College Scholarship for academic distinction; Dean's List all semesters
- Violinist in Andersen College Symphony
- Physics tutor for Bureau of Study Counsel; active participant in Habitat for Humanity
- Completed dissertation in the field of condensed matter theory

EXPERIENCE

SMART BROTHERS — New York, NY
Technology Project Manager – Investment Banking — June 2003 – July 2005
- Managed project teams to develop profit and loss systems for Proprietary Trading group
- Promoted to project leadership role in two years, well ahead of department average of four
- Developed an original mathematical algorithm for trading processing module, improving performance by 1200%
- Led team of six analysts in firmwide project to reengineer loan syndicate trading flows in firm's largest technology project of 2005. Recommendations established new firmwide standard for real-time trade processing
- Appointed lead developer of interest accrual team after just three months in department. Initiated and designed project to create customized, improved interest accrual and P&L applications for fixed income controllers
- Selected to work on high-profile project to reengineer corporate bond trading P&L system. Reduced overnight processing time from six hours to 20 minutes and improved desktop application speed by 350%
- Devoted 20-25 hours a month to instructing junior members of the team in interest accrual and trading

FINANCIAL TECHNOLOGY GROUP — New York, NY
Analyst — June 2002 – May 2003
- Developed cutting-edge analytic software for use by Wall Street traders
- Worked on a daily basis with clients to create and implement customized strategic software solution for equity traders. Helped create and deliver extensive training program for clients
- Initiated, created, and documented new firmwide standard for software module development

OTHER
- Winner of Mastermaster.com stock trading competition in November 2003. Won first place out of over 1,600 entrants worldwide with one-month return of 43.3%
- Other interests include violin, soccer, and the harmonica
- Recent travel to Yemen, Egypt, and Venezuela

CELINA M. KOCH
ckoch@state.edu
777 N. Mills Lane, Upstate, NY 14120
516-555-1974

OBJECTIVE	To obtain a position in management consulting that will leverage my operations research and economic skills.
EDUCATION	State University, Upstate, NY School of Operations Research and Industrial Engineering Candidate for Bachelor of Science Degree with a major in Operations Research, May 2006 GPA: 3.2/4.0 (3.6 in major)
DISTINCTIONS	Dean's List, State University Women in Engineering Scholarship, Texas Instruments Engineering Scholarship, National Science Foundation Research Grant
COURSES	Microeconomics; International Economics; Economic Analysis of Engineering Systems; Financial Management and Accounting; Statistics; Optimization; Engineering Management

EXPERIENCE

Research Associate Summer 2005
Ivy University, Newark, NJ
Department of Civil Engineering and Operations Research
- Used linear programming methods to model problems in international infrastructure engineering
- Generated and tested original hypothesis regarding toll-road development. Presented results to senior research scientists

Staff Technologist Summer 2004
Ring Communications Research, Belleville, NJ
Broadband Data Operations
- Analyzed Inter-Switching System Interface to determine causes and effects of packet routing issues
- Developed optimization algorithm for packet routing system. Worked with senior management to devise implementation plan

Summer Intern, Operations Research Summer 2003
Serious Instruments, Dallas, TX
Defense Systems and Electronics Group
- Assisted in implementation of new statistical process control software
- Created statistical procedure to test operating temperature of electronic defense systems. Collected and analyzed data using Excel macros. Presented findings to middle and senior managers

SKILLS	Knowledge of Microsoft PowerPoint, Excel, and Word Experienced in research methods and presentation
OTHER	Avid outdoor rock climber Proficient in German and Russian
REFERENCES	Available upon request

RACHEL O. NEWBURY
35 Howard Street, Cambridge, MA 02139
617-864-9999 • rnewbury@newton.edu

EDUCATION

Newton College Bachelor of Arts in International Economic Policy expected June 2008. Cambridge, MA • Winner of Walker Award, given to an outstanding member of the junior (Sept. 1999-present) class for academic enthusiasm and energetic participation in campus and community activities. Chosen by senior class committee.

- Winner of Haley Prize for academic excellence in Non-Western history
- Awarded citation for independent research on Kenya's Mau Mau movement.
- GPA: 3.5/4.0. GRE: 770 Math, 750 Analytical

University of Paris Study abroad during sophomore year. Paris, France • Advanced level certificate in French language and history. (Jan. 2006-May 2006)

Public High School Graduate, 1999. Salutatorian. SAT: 1450, Cleveland, OH • Principal's Award for academic and extracurricular achievement (Sept. 2000-June 2004) • Duke of Edinburgh's Award for involvement in community service.

WORK EXPERIENCE

The Community Center Worked closely with programming staff in organizing interdisciplinary seminars (Non-Profit) for international experts in development and cultural studies. Vienna, Austria • Researched and prepared program materials on diverse subjects such as Summer Intern Public Health, Urbanization, Asian Economies and Agro-technology (June 2006-Aug. 2006) • Promoted interactions among participants in academic and social settings.

Newton Campus Society Organized weekly student discussions on public policy issues. Intern • Identified current issues for debate and prepared topic briefings Sept. 2000-Present • Trained student facilitators to lead small group discussions

Mass Realty State realtor education and licensing organization. Boston, MA • Designed, implemented, and maintained database of over 6,000 Summer Intern companies for programming efforts (June 2000-Aug. 2000) • Successfully trained entire organization in usage of new database

Campus Volunteer Office Coordinated publicity and recruitment efforts. Program Assistant • Redesigned publicity materials for over thirty community service Sept. 2004-May 2005 programs.

- Solicited articles, edited and designed quarterly newsletter for volunteers.
- Coordinated 200 student volunteers in one-day cultural event for over 300 underprivileged children in local region.

EXTRA-CURRICULAR ACTIVITIES

The Newton Daily Member of editorial board of widely-circulated campus daily newspaper. Editor • Edited or copy-edited two out of five issues every week • Initiated and conducted interviews with many distinguished visitors

Amnesty International Active member of international human rights organization for seven years. Member • Surpervised funding efforts and coordinated events for college chapter
Member of national advisory council on fundraising strategies

- Installed permanent human rights murals in subway station
- Personally raised over $50,000 for group activities.

COMPUTER SKILLS Word, Excel, Powerpoint, Pagemaker, Photoshop and Filemaker

OTHER INTERESTS Photography, ballroom dancing, and horseback riding.

Undergraduate Informational Interview Letter

Samuel Song
76 Trombone Way
Chicago, IL 60610
ssong126@yahoo.com

October 1, 2007

Jim Smith, Manager
Prestige Consulting
100 N. Michigan Ave., 29th Floor
Chicago, IL 60606

Dear Mr. Smith:

My name is Samuel Song. I am a senior at Public University majoring in government, and I am extremely interested in a career in consulting. I found you listed in our school's alumni database as an employee of Prestige Consulting.

I would like to find out more about a career in strategy consulting, and more specifically, how Prestige Consulting differs from the other firms in its approach to consulting. It would benefit me a great deal if I could meet with you for about 30 minutes to discuss a few of these issues and to get a feel for life as a consultant, particularly at Prestige Consulting. I know that you were in a position similar to mine not long ago, and I would certainly appreciate your insights on your success in gaining a position at an outstanding firm.

I would love to meet with you on Wednesday, October 9 or Thursday, October 10. If you are able to meet with me on either of those days, I would greatly appreciate it. I know you are extremely busy, and I would be delighted to meet with you on another day that works for you. In addition, if you feel there are any other consultants in your office that would be beneficial for me to talk to at that time, I would love to set up meetings with them as well.

Thank you very much for your time. I will follow up with you by phone on Thursday, October 3.

Sincerely,

Samuel Song

Undergraduate Application Letter

Salley Kooman
1 Diamond Street
Los Angeles, CA 90012

October 31, 2007

Ted Schenkel, Recruiting Coordinator
West Coast Partners
7 Main St., 43 Floor
Los Angeles, CA 90015

Dear Mr. Schenkel:

I am a senior at California University majoring in English, and I am extremely interested in position with West Coast Partners upon graduation.

Consulting is definitely the career I want to pursue. Work on my dissertation to this point has involved extensive research, hypothesis formulation, hours of analysis, and team collaboration with my mentor; this process is not unlike the consulting project cycle. In addition, my elective coursework in microeconomics has increased my interest and honed my skills in the business arena. A series of conversations with consultants at various firms – especially West Coast Partners – has confirmed that consulting is the right career for me.

West Coast Partners appeals to me for a number of reasons. I am extremely interested in the life sciences and telecom industries, and West Coast Partners is particularly strong in those industries. I am also drawn to the small size of the firm, as I feel it would create more immediate opportunities for leadership and a strong community environment. Finally, I have been incredibly impressed with all of the consultants I've spoken with from your firm; each person is bright yet humble, passionate yet and good-natured. I would be thrilled to join your firm.

I have enclosed my resume for your review. I very much appreciate your time and consideration, and I hope to hear from your team in the near future.

Sincerely,

Salley Kooman

MBA Summer Internship Letter

February 1, 2007

Kimberly Sharpe, Recruiting Manager
Hexagonal Consulting
666 Avenue of the Americas
13th Floor
New York, NY

Dear Ms. Sharpe,

I am a first year MBA student at State Business School. I was extremely impressed with Hexagonal Consulting's approach to management consulting after attending the presentation given by your firm earlier this quarter. I also learned more about your firm by talking with William Field and several other summer interns. My discussions with them confirmed my interest in Hexagonal Consulting, and I am now writing to request an invitation to interview for a summer associate consulting position.

After graduating from Northern College with a degree in accounting, I worked as an associate in the Finance department of AutoCo, a well-known automotive manufacturer. I gained solid analytical and problem solving skills there. I was responsible for identifying and resolving financial reporting issues, as well as generating innovative methods to improve our processes. I also fine-tuned my communication and consensus building skills, as I often needed to present and market my work to middle and upper management. Finally, during my last year of employment, I took on a team leadership role, managing the daily work of five junior members of our team and taking an active role in our training for new hires.

I am excited by the strong potential fit I see with Hexagonal Consulting. I feel that the analytical, leadership and teamwork abilities gained through my employment and academic experience have provided me with the tools and skills necessary to perform well in a consulting career, and will allow me to make a significant contribution at your firm. I am particularly intrigued by the shareholder value focus of Hexagonal Consulting's methodology, since it fits well with my experience in finance.

I have enclosed my resume for your review. I welcome the opportunity to meet with you when you recruit at SBS for summer internships later this month, and I would greatly appreciate being included on your invitational list.

Thank you for your time and consideration. I look forward to hearing from you.

Sincerely,

Laura Haley
314 Broadway, Apt. 15
New York, NY 10007
lbethhaley@hotmail.com

MBA Full-Time Letter

Ms. Margaret Jones, Recruiting Manager
Mainstream Consulting Group
123 21st Street
Boston, Massachusetts 02145

August 19, 2007

Dear Ms. Jones:

It was a pleasure to meet you in person last week at the Mainstream Consulting invitational lunch on the Boston Business School campus. Having spoken with your colleagues at the event, I believe that Mainstream would be an exciting and challenging firm in which to build my career.

My background fits well with a position in strategy consulting. As a Midway University physics undergraduate, I developed an analytic, creative mind geared towards solving complex problems. I applied and enhanced my problem solving skills as a technology project leader at Smart Brothers Investment Bank, where I focused on making business processes faster, more effective, and more efficient. Creating these results for traders, financial analysts, and senior management taught me how to effectively partner with clients throughout the various phases of business transformation. In addition, I gained valuable team leadership experience at Smart Brothers, guiding many project teams through the successful design and implementation of cutting-edge technology strategies.

As a telecommunications strategy intern at Global Consulting Associates this summer, I confirmed that strategy consulting is indeed the right career for me. Our project team helped a major telecommunications provider formulate a wireless data services strategy. I led the industry analysis and market opportunity assessment. This experience showed me that I am an effective contributor in a consulting environment, where industry knowledge, creative problem solving skills, fact-based analysis, and client focus are rewarded.

Mainstream appeals to me over other firms because of its focus on pure strategy projects, small firm atmosphere, and accelerated career growth opportunities. Please consider me for your invitational campus interviews this fall. I am particularly interested in positions in the San Francisco and Chicago offices, and I have enclosed my resume for your review.

Thank you for your time, and I look forward to hearing from you soon.

Sincerely,

Michael A. Thomas
100 Wellany Way
Boston, MA 02111
michaelt3@bostonu.edu

Building and Maintaining a Network

Good networking skills are important throughout your career, but these skills are immensely helpful in opening doors to your favorite firms. You need to work especially hard at networking in a difficult economic climate, as a contact typically goes a lot further than a blind e-mail.

Generating a network from scratch

As a rule, large consulting firms only conduct on-campus recruiting at some eight to 10 schools, and smaller consulting firms might target just three to six schools. These institutions are usually the highest-ranked ones, plus those that key partners attended, and possibly a lesser-ranked one in a city with a major firm office. Whether you attend one of the schools that will be graced by a firm's on-campus presence or not, having a personal contact with the firm is an important way to get noticed.

Find a contact within the firms you are targeting, be it an alumnus/a, a colleague who worked there prior to school, your mother's best friend or anyone else. If you truly have no contacts, then go ahead and call up the recruiter listed on the company's web site, identify yourself and express your interest in the firm.

You could then ask the contact for an informational interview. An informational interview is just that—a short discussion to gather more information about the firm. It can take place in person (which is preferable) or on the phone. Use the informational interview for two purposes—to get an "in" on the recruiting process and to learn more about the company prior to your interviews. Asking for an informational interview is often a more innocuous approach than asking for a regular interview outright. If you can't get an informational interview with a consultant in person, try for one over the phone. Firms aren't always looking for new employees, but most are always interested in selling their firm to others and generating publicity and goodwill.

Managing your contacts

We all have friends who just seem to know everyone. They know what others are up to and are a great resource for the best parties in town. They make networking and schmoozing look easy. But networking is hard, even for them. It takes a lot of effort to maintain a contact.

The key to networking is consistent follow-up. After a great conversation, you need to make sure you've locked an impression of yourself in that person's mind. A quick e-mail is an easy and acceptable way to do this. Simply reintroduce yourself, remind them of a few key things you talked about, and thank them again for their time. If someone did something particularly nice for you (like introduced you to a partner with special expertise in your area of interest), send him or her a thank-you note.

Continue to check in with your contacts throughout the process, especially if they are consultants. While it's great to stay in touch with the human resources staff because they manage the hiring process, an endorsement by someone already working in the firm goes a long way. There is no real science to how often to call your contacts; your goal is to stay on the firm's radar without being overaggressive. Twice a month should be fine.

Good networkers also think ahead to when they might want to get touch with the person next. For example, if the closed interview list deadline is next month, pencil in a day to call up your favorite contact at the firm for advice on the cover letter. Perhaps they will remember you and call the recruiting consultants to recommend you as someone with strong potential. In general, the more people you know in a particular organization, the greater your chances of success.

Notes for on-campus recruiting

If you have a strong on-campus recruiting program at your school, you're in luck. Make sure you attend the appropriate company presentations—you may be asked whether you attended the presentations at your interview, and in any case it's a great way to make contacts. (Here's one hint: Approach consultants before the presentation when they have time, rather than after the presentation when they are sure to be mobbed.) Be sure to get from your career services office a list of all of the recruiting consulting companies, the date and time of their on-campus information session, the dates of the first round interviews and the names of the appropriate contacts. Build a spreadsheet or list of target companies with all of this information so you can keep track of the process.

Most firms offer an information session where partners deliver an overview presentation of the firm and you can speak with current consultants. We strongly recommend you attend this session. You will be able to confirm your overall impression of the firm and its specific application process, and it's a great way to generate nominal contacts at each firm. Definitely try to speak with the current consultants and ask about what they do on the job and how they like it, and don't forget to get the business card of those you felt you connected with. If you spoke with someone for a long time, a good technique is to follow up with an e-mail to thank them for their time. You can then call with further questions. (Tip: These sessions often offer free food and cocktails. Even though it's free, don't go overboard! Trust us, the firms really remember those who did.)

Other thoughts on networking

Truly effective networking involves developing longer-term relationships for both parties' benefit. You begin these relationships with the goal of seeking a mutually beneficial outcome. You find people with whom you can exchange ideas, favors and politics. Eventually, you find people who will support you even when you do not need it. They actively become involved in your life, and vice versa.

Extroverts generally find networking easier, because approaching strangers comes more naturally to them. Introverts can be outstanding networkers, but tend to be more selective about whom they approach. Either way, think of networking and relationship-building as a lifestyle you constantly want to improve. The more relationships you develop, the more fruitful you will find your career. Working on your network will also test out whether you're cut out for a partner position in the long run; after all, the partner track is all about sales, and many of your future client accounts will emerge from your valuable network.

Applying to the Firm

Now the fun part: the actual application.

Entry points and when to apply

Typically, new consulting hires comes fresh out of school and start in the fall. At most firms, there are two non-partner entry points (we discuss these roles plus that of the partner later in this book):

- Those just having earned an undergraduate degree. This position is usually called "business analyst," and involves activities like data gathering, basic data analysis and presentation development.

- Those just having earned a graduate degree, typically (but not necessarily limited to) an MBA. This position is usually titled "consultant" or "associate" and involves heavy client interaction, quantitative modeling, presentation structuring and development, and limited project management.

The timing of the hiring process can vary depending on the stage of growth of each consulting firm:

- Large, established consulting firms that can predict their staffing needs a year from now, with some accuracy, follow a recruiting cycle with interviews in the fall for the following fall. (Sometimes this is known as hiring "ahead of the curve".) At many top-caliber institutions, both undergraduate and graduate, such firms will enter the on-campus recruiting program that enables them to select candidates for first-round interviews using that school's centralized application pool. This is highly convenient for firms with high turnover that need a steady influx of candidates and with historical success hiring from specific target schools.

- On the other hand, smaller, less-established consulting firms usually have a more variable project pipeline and can't predict hiring needs as easily. Therefore, these firms don't always follow the fall-to-fall recruiting cycle. Some of them will follow this cycle anyway because strong graduating candidates will be making job decisions in the late fall or early winter and the smaller firms want to make sure their offers are considered in parallel. But many of these smaller firms hire much closer to when they think they will need to staff up (or "behind the curve").

So, if you're looking for a post-school job, start researching prospective employers the summer before your last year in school, and enter the on-campus recruiting system that fall. Keep in mind that not all compelling consulting firms, large or small, choose to recruit on campus (primarily because doing so is pretty expensive), so be sure to include off-campus recruiting in your job search.

Writing the cover letter

Firms vary on the importance of the cover letter. Some recruiters don't read it and go straight to the resume. Others look at it as a true writing sample. Don't take any chances; take the cover letter seriously.

There are some standard components to cover letters in consulting. We aren't recommending that you follow this outline slavishly, but we do think you should include them all in some form:

- **Introduction**—Identify your current position or school standing, and express your general interest in the firm.

- **Relevant experience**—Discuss how your background and experience fits consulting. If the firm has a specialty, explain how and why you are interested in that specialty.

- **Interest in consulting**—Discuss (briefly) what aspects of consulting appeal to you. Is it the problem-solving? The variety? Your love of assisting clients?

- **Interest in the firm**—Why do you want to work for this firm?

- **Additional information**—Depending on the preference of the company, you may need to include information such as your preferred start date and office location. Be sure to list more than one office location if possible, because some firms have office-specific hiring needs and you might increase your chances of getting hired if you list more than one office.

- **Next steps**—If you are applying through your school, the next steps are usually clear. (On campus, the recruiter will normally invite selected students to interview; some schools have a lottery system for interviews as well. If you are unfamiliar with how interviewers are assigned at your school, contact your career guidance counselor.) Otherwise, you will need to specify the next form of contact. We suggest you write in your letter that you will follow up with the recruiter in a few days to discuss what happens next.

- **Closing**—Be sure to thank the reader for his or her consideration and time.

Be sure to proofread; we've all heard stories of cover letters to Accenture that begin, "I'm very interested in a position with Bain & Company." This actually happens more often than you think at the undergraduate and MBA level. Students often apply to up to 20 companies at once, so there's a high chance of a mistake slipping through the cracks. Triple-check everything. The consulting market is so competitive that the slightest error may sink your application. You may want to have a friend read your cover letters too.

Most of all, keep the cover letter to one page. It takes a lot of effort to make the letter both concise and powerful, and it will be worth the effort.

Additional materials

Most firms only want to see the cover letter and resume, but you should confirm that they don't have any special requirements. BCG, for example, wants to see your SAT scores and transcript. You will want to check what other requirements specific firms have for your resume or cover, including GPA or GMAT on the resume or office preference in the cover letter. Ask the firm's recruiting manager for these details.

Sending it in

More firms these days request that candidates apply by e-mail. This is fine. Most of the time, you can send the cover letter as e-mail text and attach your resume in Microsoft Word format. We advise you to confirm this format with your recruiter contact.

If you need to send a paper version, print your materials on nicely-woven resume paper stock using a laser printer. Paper clips are preferred to staples.

Following up

It is generally a good idea to check in with the recruiter and make sure your application was received. A quick e-mail is fine and will do the trick. Campus recruiters are usually good about responding, because they know that the process is stressful.

Most firms have "core" schools they prioritize. If you are not from one of those core schools, or if you have already graduated, you will often have a more difficult time hearing back from the companies of your choice. Don't give up—keep contacting the firm if you are truly interested. Consulting firms appreciate follow-through.

Lateral Hires

Most consultants get into the business directly out of either undergraduate school or graduate school (and less often, directly at a principal level after a long career in industry). The firms actively recruit on select campuses, and hire whole "classes" of new consultants, which gradually get winnowed down over the years through attrition to other industries and layoffs. Generally, management consulting firms have no need to add new employees partway up their pyramid structure—their problem is more about how to slim down the ranks as they gain seniority, in order to avoid the profitability hit of being too top-heavy.

That said, there are increasing numbers of so-called 'lateral hires' into consulting firms. This refers to two sets of people: (1) consultants working at one firm who switch to another firm, and (2) people working in an industry other than consulting for some or many years after graduation who switch into consulting. Worming your way into the field of consulting as a student is difficult enough, and getting in as a lateral hire involves even longer odds. Lateral hires are far more common among smaller and less prominent firms—the large, name-brand consultancies have tended to cultivate exclusivity by keeping folks out who presumably didn't make the cut during campus recruiting. But, even the big guns have experimented more and more with lateral hiring over the past few years. In the 2001-2003 economic downturn, consulting firms made dramatic workforce cuts, only to find five years later that they have unacceptable gaps in their mid-level ranks. Those underpopulated new MBA classes from half a decade ago emerged into now underpopulated senior manager classes, thus creating demand for lateral hires at that level. A similar line of thinking applies for postgraduate degree lateral hires—it's not uncommon for an MBA with two years of post-graduate industry experience to jump into a consulting firm as first-year associate.

That trend appears to be continuing, with firms having learned that lateral hires can work out well. And, of course, the smaller, less famous firms, and highly specialized firms have always looked for prospective employees among qualified professionals of all ages and years of experience.

Now, if you haven't gone back for grad school yet, don't think that working for two years somewhere and being a lateral hire is a back-door way to getting ahead in consulting without the MBA. If you've worked a couple of years out of undergrad and switch over to a mainstream consulting firm, chances are that you will "start over" at the new business analyst level. You may think it unfair that firms may not "credit" you for your years of experience, but realize that the firm needs to invest quite a bit of time in your learning its "system" of consulting—just like they invest time in new undergrads—and everyone is better positioned for success if you start as an analyst versus a consultant or associate. Some firms have a senior analyst position that is reserved for business analysts after a couple of years at that firm, and if you have relevant industry knowledge or are coming from another consulting firm, you might get placed into that role. And, ultimately, if you don't have an MBA, you may very well be encouraged or forced to leave and go get one anyway, regardless of the extra experience you bring in the door. A similar line of thinking applies for postgraduate degree lateral hires—it's not uncommon for an MBA to work two years after graduation in industry, then jump into a large consulting firms as a first-year associate.

Laterally-hired consultants report that it feels a bit humiliating to backslide a few years in their career progression, as they end up working side-by-side with someone fresh out of school who may not have any work experience, or even working for someone with fewer years of work experience. But, that is just the way the system works, and if you want to be a management consultant badly enough, it can certainly be worth the setback.

The biggest problem lateral hires seem to face is finding a balance between bringing their existing experience and maturity to the table (which is, after all, why they were hired), and yet being appropriately deferential and politically sensitive around supervisors who may be their own age or younger. Indeed, lateral hires are fundamentally between a rock and a hard place in this respect. We've heard countless stories of people excited to join a consulting firm from another firm or from a corporate job, only to find that their new colleagues resent them—the (irrational and erroneous) perception is that the lateral hire was handed something she didn't earn. You could be hired for your project management experience and given a project to manage, but then easily be deemed too aggressive if you don't take care to show proper deference and humility. If you are hired laterally into a mid-level or management-level position, this is by definition hard to do.

Getting hired laterally involves much longer odds than going for a spot in a first-year consulting class through on-campus recruiting. So, if you go this route, make sure you are just as prepared as those MBAs who study cases for months prior to their interviews. There is no standardized lateral hiring process—it is just done as needed and without much advertising. So you can apply basically at any time of the year, and apply to firms "on spec" without necessarily knowing that they are looking for someone at your level. But keep in mind that the bulk of normal-cycle full-time hiring decisions occur each fall, so try to time your application to the on-campus recruiting cycles. Once your application is in, there are a number of ways the process could unfold. If you are fairly close in experience level to a new undergraduate or new MBA hire, your interviews and evaluations will likely be nearly identical to those of a student applicant. If you have a few more years of experience, many firms forgo the typical, formal interview process and opt for a series of conversations instead—if you have several years of good post-MBA experience after going to a good school, the evaluation becomes far more about your project experience and your cultural fit than your ability to recollect case frameworks from years ago.

GO FOR THE GOLD!

GET VAULT GOLD MEMBERSHIP AND GET ACCESS TO ALL OF VAULT'S AWARD-WINNING CONSULTING CAREER INFORMATION

◆ **Employee surveys** for top consulting firms, with insider info on
  - Company culture
  - Salaries and compensation
  - Hiring process and interviews
  - Business outlook

◆ Access to **100+ extended insider consulting firm profiles**

◆ **Vault's exclusive consulting firm rankings,** including quality of life and practice area rankings

◆ Insider consulting salary information with **Vault's Consulting Salary Central**

◆ **Student and alumni surveys** for 100s of top MBA programs and law schools

◆ Access to **complete Vault message board archives**

◆ **15% off** all Vault purchases, including Vault Guides, Consulting Employer Profiles and Case Interview Prep

For more information go to
www.vault.com/consulting

> the most trusted name in career informa

The Interview

CHAPTER 5

What to Expect in the Interview

If all goes well, you will land a few interviews. The following is a typical format for the consulting interview process:

- Preliminary phone screen: A half-hour conversation with an HR professional or a consultant (sometimes a partner, sometimes a junior consultant) to do a sanity check on whether you should be interviewed or not. This step is optional but is happening more and more to save valuable time by actually interviewing fewer candidates.

- 1st round: One or two half-hour interviews with a senior consultant. Expect at least one of these interviews to contain a case.

- 2nd round: Up to four 45-minute interviews. You can expect that all of these will be case interviews. At least one of these interviews probably will be with a partner, as many firms will not hire a candidate unless partners have spoken with the candidate. Most firms extend offers after the second round. If the candidate has requested a specific office, the interviews will most likely take place in that office. Otherwise, the candidate will interview at the nearest regional office or in a hotel.

- 3rd round: In infrequent cases, firms will ask candidates back for a third round of interviews, often exclusively with partners of the firm.

Consulting interviews fall into two types: the behavioral interview and the case/problem interview. The former determines the extent to which you fit the consultant profile and the firm's culture. The latter tests your problem-solving skills and displays your thinking patterns to the interviewer. To an extent, both types of interviews also reveal how well you deal with stressful real-time challenges. Candidates at the undergraduate level might receive brainteasers and "guesstimates" instead of cases. MBA and advanced degree candidates typically are not asked directly to solve a brainteaser or do a guesstimate, though an estimate of industry market size might appear within a case. (For more case interview practice, please refer to the *Vault Guide to the Case Interview* and both volumes of the *Vault Case Interview Practice Guide*, available on the Vault web site and in traditional bookstores.)

The Resume/Behavioral Interview

Interviewers first want to determine if you have the "mental horsepower" (brains) and "quantitative and analytical ability" (math and logic skills) to be an asset. You must also be able to think "out of the box" (creatively) to come up with innovative ideas and approaches.

While your resume provides structure for the interview, be sure your side of the conversation provides more than a regurgitation of the resume's key points. Focus on the same skills you underscored in your resume, but use different examples of teamwork, leadership, confidence and technical skills. Show them that the examples on your resume do not constitute the entirety of your abilities. Interviewers take on the responsibility of shaping their firm's culture and/or ensuring compliance with firm standards. Generally, consulting firms want smart, ambitious, hardworking, dedicated and analytical people with pleasant demeanors.

During the interview, pay attention to what you say and how you say it. Listen carefully to the questions. Too many people lose points by answering the questions incorrectly, incompletely or inappropriately. Make your answers logical and structured. Provide relevant examples. Speak in complete sentences, and do not go off on tangents or trail off midway through a sentence. Also, watch your fillers: "you know," "um" and "like." Ensure that you speak eloquently.

Some specific skills and qualities that interviewers look for:

- Leadership skills to lead consulting and client teams and to promote your ideas
- Teamwork to work with other consultants, clients and vendors toward solutions
- Analytical skills to crunch numbers and work through information in a logical manner
- Presentation skills to communicate findings to fellow consultants and clients alike
- Creativity to solve problems and think "out of the box"
- Thick skin for those times when your work is criticized
- Personality and sense of humor to diffuse stressful situations

During your interviews, remember these specific points:

- Never express uncertainty or insecurity about your skills or give the interviewer any reason to question your confidence or abilities
- Refrain from revealing your dislike for travel or your attachment to home
- Avoid getting defensive or sensitive when answering tough questions, including: "What people do you have trouble getting along with?" Another favorite: "Tell us about your shortcomings"

During your interview, be prepared for some version of the "airplane test." The interviewer imagines sitting next to you on an eight-hour flight across the Atlantic. She or he decides which is more preferable: Conversing with you for more than 30 seconds or faking sleep throughout the whole flight to avoid you altogether. To pass the test, show genuine interest in something outside the business realm or crack a clean joke. Just be sure to choose a topic that presents you as mature, insightful and interesting and make certain that the topic is tasteful, amusing and noncontroversial. (For related topics, see the section "Interview Questions That Never Get Asked (But Are Always Answered.")

Behavioral Questions

Consulting firms use "behavioral interview questions" to measure "softer" attributes. Behavioral interview questions ask you to reveal how you behave in particular situations, be it at work or in a personal situation. Firms using behavioral interviews believe a candidate's responses reveal a lot about personality and skills. They also believe the firm can project future behavioral patterns based on the past. Some consulting firms use behavioral questions almost to the exclusion of more traditional consulting case questions. To prepare, practice answering the more frequently asked behavioral questions until you can answer them smoothly.

Practice Behavioral Interview Questions

When asking behavioral questions, your interviewer first listens to your answers at face value and then assesses your thinking process (ingesting the question, processing the answer, assembling the words and presenting the answer). They also use their assessment to project the likelihood of your success as a consultant.

1. How do you deal with someone in your group who isn't pulling his or her weight, or disagrees with your goals?

Avoid criticism. Try to think of a time when you encouraged someone to do his or her best or won someone over to your side. Team sports examples are good here. Emphasize how everyone has something to contribute.

2. What position do you normally take on a team?

Avoid portraying yourself as an obsequious follower or a tyrannical dictator. Consulting firms want people (especially neophytes) who ask questions, make contributions and get their points across. They want someone who neither passively receives information nor commandeers the entire case team.

3. Tell me what you're most proud of on your resume.

Choose something that conveys the qualities consulting firms want and that lets you explain something not obvious to the interviewer. (Because many consulting firms have international branches, discussing a study abroad program or an international position might win you points.)

4. How have you shown leadership in the past?

Consulting firms like candidates who show strong managerial potential, and they like to see evidence of your leadership skills. Speak of leadership roles you took during college, such as co-chair of a fund-raising event.

Many aspiring consultants have not had specific leadership roles. If you have work experience, describe a time you took initiative, such as created a training program for junior team members or convinced the management to switch from DOS to Windows. If you haven't, talk about proactive efforts you made in your student groups. The point is to show initiative; past leadership positions are a proxy for this, but you will do just as well by describing key experiences.

5. Why have you chosen to interview at our firm?

Consulting involves a lot of research. Show off your skills here. Explain your interest in a strategy firm (or change management, or whatever), and relate your interest to what you know of the firm. Include what you want to gain from the firm and what you believe you can contribute. State why the firm stands in a good position to accomplish your goals and how the firm can benefit from your contributions. Demonstrate your abilities to weave data from separate sources into a single analysis.

6. What is the worst mistake you've ever made?

Do not cite an egregious lapse in judgment along the lines of: "It was really stupid of me to violate parole." Instead, describe a valuable lesson you learned (preferably some time ago). Remember to include your lesson and why the lesson holds value to you even today. "I remember when I didn't fully research buying a car, and I ended up buying a car that looked good but cost me thousands in repairs. I'll never fail to do my homework again."

7. Why should we not hire you?

Leave out any actual flaws unknown to your interviewer. Instead, explain why something that looks like a weakness actually represents a strength (or at worst, something neutral). "I can understand that you would potentially be put off by my lack of economics and business coursework. But I think my sales experience and my score of 770 on the math portion of the SAT should alleviate those concerns."

The Case Interview

Consulting interviewers use interview questions to test your analytical ability, reasoning skills, confidence and knowledge of business concepts. Case interviews simulate live scenarios to test your mind's quickness and confirm the skills you claim on your resume. You must discuss hypothetical situations based on information provided to you and make assumptions based on commonly-known facts. Even if you have no background knowledge of the case, you must still address the question thoughtfully under pressure. The interviewer cares more about how you arrived at your answer than if you answer correctly, so be sure to explain your thought process too.

Case interview questions fall into three broad categories: business cases, guesstimates and brainteasers.

Business cases

If you are interviewing with a strategy consulting firm, count on plenty of cases during the interview process. Put very simply, case interviews are problem-solving exercises. While some interviewers draw on recent real-world experience to develop a case, you are not expected to have any industry knowledge. The interviewer is more interested in checking out your thought process and assessing your analytical ability, creativity and poise. Some companies present cases as written documents to be read and prepared. But usually, the interviewer describes the key facts and issues of the case before asking the candidate for an analysis. Several firms (e.g., Monitor) ask you to solve a case as part of a team with other job candidates.

The case usually consists of a business scenario and a question about it. For example: "A foreign company with extra cash on hand wants to enter the American fast food market. What would you tell them?" While every case is different, follow the tips below to improve your chances of cracking it without too much difficulty.

Some quick case tips

- Before jumping into an answer, ask the interviewer a number of questions to gather vital information about the case. Your interviewer will answer you with pieces of information to help you formulate new questions and, ultimately, your case recommendations. (At the same time, avoid tiring your interviewer and recognize when you have asked enough questions. If your interviewer starts repeating himself or herself or says something like, "You should be able to give me an answer," stop asking questions.)

- One interviewee cautions: "Consulting firms are looking for people who will think carefully before answering; this is very important in the case interview. Don't say the first thing that comes to your mind, even if you're certain about it. If you're trying to choose between appearing to be slow and appearing to be a cocky idiot, choose the former."

- Ask about best practices in the industry. Find out what other companies in this industry do when facing similar issues.

- Avoid making assumptions without checking them with the interviewer, or at the very least, state that you are making an assumption. If your case concerns a major vehicle manufacturer, you might mistakenly assume the client is General Motors, Ford or Toyota, when it is actually John Deere.

- After gathering all the information you think you need, start formulating your recommendations. If you like using standard frameworks, remember to use the appropriate one. Run the framework through your mind to ensure you are not forgetting a vital area of analysis. For instance, the Porter's Five Forces model might help you analyze a market situation and identify all of the areas of potential threat. Based on the model, you can recommend the company's market strategy.

- If you are unfamiliar with frameworks, state so and proceed as logically as you are able. Voice your analysis—why and how you come to your questions and conclusions is also important.

- After giving your recommendations, consider pointing out possible flaws and assumptions in your thinking. If it's clear you really didn't do well on the case, you might try explaining how you would have approached it differently given the chance.

- Speak and reason aloud during your case interview. Your thought process is more important than your ultimate conclusions; your interviewer must hear your reasoning and the logical steps you are taking to reach your conclusions.

- Always bring paper and a reliable pen with you to any consulting interview. You might want to take notes during the case interview (and for any guesstimates or quantitative brainteasers your interviewer might throw at you). Asking your interviewer for paper and a pen during the interview gives the impression that you are disorganized and unprepared.

- Everyone gets stuck in a case interview at some point. One tactic is to simply admit you are stuck and try thinking out loud through the problem again. "I don't seem to be getting anywhere with this line of thinking, so I'm going to back up and think through things from the beginning." You can also just ask your interviewer for help: "I have a lot of good information in front of me, but I seem to be running into a dead end here. Maybe you could help me talk through the problem." These alternatives are both a lot better than staying silent; after all, this is exactly what would happen if you were working on a real project together and you needed help.

- No matter what, never show any signs of being flustered in a case interview. Remember to breathe! Your composure before your client (or lack thereof) is a key factor of your evaluation.

Sample Qualitative Case Questions

1) A major film entertainment company wants us to assist them in building a distribution network for home video. They want to know whether they should build their own distribution network or continue to contract with third parties.

Start by asking your interviewer some basic questions:

- What are other entertainment companies doing?
- What are the current costs?
- Does the company have the staff and resources to create its own distribution network?
- Of the major entertainment companies producing videos, do most distribute through their proprietary supply chains or through third parties?
- What is the client's current cost of distribution through its contractual partner(s)?
- Has the client considered building its own distribution network before retaining us? If so, what were its findings?
- Does the client have a dedicated functional staff assigned to the project? If so, what functional areas do they represent?

After establishing some basic facts, ask more detailed questions. Your interviewer might allude to certain avenues to discuss or shut down others. If the interviewer confirms the company has enough staff to handle setting up its network, stop delving into the ramifications of reassigning personnel.

If, through questioning, you decide that staying with a third-party distributor makes the most sense, ask the next logical question: Should the company stay with its current distributor or choose a new one?

- Who are possible alternative partners? Who uses them?
- Could you characterize the relationship between the client's distribution partner and the client? Is there a possibility of retaliation on the part of the distribution partner if the client severs its ties to this party?
- How many weeks of supply are currently in the distribution partner's pipeline?
- How receptive are the client's accounts to changing distribution partners? Has a value proposition been created to show that a client-owned supply chain would be more efficient or valuable to the accounts?

- Does the client have any financial interest in the distribution partner that might have to be severed?

When you feel ready, make a recommendation. You might be asked a more qualitative case question as well. (Recruiting insiders tell Vault that undergraduates and graduate candidates without MBAs are more likely to receive qualitative cases.) Qualitative business cases determine if you can discuss a company intelligently and analytically and use business concepts and terminology naturally in conversation.

2) We've seen a lot of consolidation in the pharmaceuticals industry over the last 10 years. What factors do you think drive this activity?

You don't have to know anything about the pharmaceutical industry or even companies like Pfizer or GlaxoSmithKline to do well with this question. On the other hand, you want to show that you can think through a complex industry using some basic analytic thinking. (Still, we recommend that you read *The Wall Street Journal* on a daily basis in the weeks before your interviews.)

If you are unfamiliar with the pharmaceutical industry—and if you are, you can say so to your interviewer without penalty—ask some questions to orient yourself. What exactly do pharmaceutical companies make? How large is the industry? How do products originate? Are there a few major players or is the industry more fragmented? How do consumers choose among different drugs that offer a similar treatment?

At a very high level, you should be able to ascertain or confirm the following pieces of information:

- Pharmaceutical companies develop and market drugs that help people with a wide variety of medical conditions, such as cancer, influenza or nasal congestion.

- Given the recent consolidation, the industry is dominated by several large players. The list includes Pfizer, GlaxoSmithKline and Bristol Myers Squibb.

- Pharma companies have increased recent usage of direct-to-consumer ads to market their drugs. One major reason for this shift is that in 1997, the Food and Drug Administration (FDA) relaxed its restrictions on the extent to which pharmaceutical companies could advertise on the airwaves, particularly television and radio.

- Market research suggests that direct-to-consumer ads have been fairly effective. Consumers are indeed requesting prescription drugs and purchasing over-the-counter drugs on the basis of advertising.
- All new drugs undergo several expensive stages of testing by the FDA before they can come to market.
- Few drugs pass all phases of FDA testing. Successful drugs take many years (six to ten) to complete the full cycle of testing.
- Drugs can be patented, but most patents expire in 17 years. At this point, the drug will be subject to generic competitors. Many drugs are patented before the full cycle of FDA testing finishes.
- While all of the major pharmaceutical companies have their own R&D departments, most partner with biotechnology companies, which specialize in the research and development of new life science technologies. Biotech firms usually restrict their attention to the discovery and preclinical stages of the R&D process, and the pharmaceutical companies carry the drug through the last stages of FDA test.

A good answer to this question might suggest that mergers are either revenue-enhancing or cost-reducing to the parties involved.

- *Revenue-enhancing*—One company might buy another because it wants access to a larger revenue base. When its patent expires, a drug becomes subject to generic competitors, and the drug will make less money for its parent company. This is why drug companies are constantly on the prowl for new drugs to develop.
- *Cost-reducing*—A big reason for pharma companies to merge is to save costs. Many companies save money by combining overhead and R&D expenses and reducing headcount. Sales and marketing are enormous expenditures for pharma companies.

An even better answer would incorporate some more advanced reasons.

- Mergers in the pharma industry can reduce risk because the combined drug pipeline will be larger. Very few drugs in the R&D stage pass the FDA tests and make it to market. Each stage of FDA testing (Phase I/II/III) has a historically low probability of success, so if one multiplies out the probabilities, there is a very low overall probability of success for any given drug. So, a pharma company wants to have as many products in development as possible to ensure that a few will make it to market and that perhaps one over a given timeframe will become a real hit.

- A company might want to capture the revenue from a competitor's winning drug. For example, Pfizer purchased Warner-Lambert mainly for its leading drug, Lipitor. Pfizer also made a bid to purchase Pharmacia largely because of Pharmacia's strength in oncology.
- Companies might also merge because of irrationality. Companies in the 1990s believed that scaling up was the way to go.
- Because marketing and brand awareness is so important, a larger pharma company can join two strong brand names with joint advertising and create an even larger market power than the two companies individually could have had before.

3) A restaurant owner is setting up a new restaurant and making some basic decisions on the layout. He is making a decision on the facilities to place in the restrooms for customers to dry their hands. Initial research suggests that he has three options—paper towels, roller towels and hot air dryers. He needs to decide today. What should he consider in his decision making process?

In the initial analysis, ask a number of questions that will influence your decision.

- What type of restaurant is it going to be—luxury, moderate or cheap?
- How many customers does he expect? How many tables? Is it open during the day? In the evening?
- Has he done any customer research to see what customers would prefer?

Fairly soon in the process, start asking about the economics of the three options. Expect the interviewer to give you more information:

In the initial research, the restaurant owner found the following information from the suppliers of the drying facilities:

- Dryers have an initial cost of $500 each (but you need two—one for each restroom) and a total monthly service charge of $100 per month. The supplier estimates that the lifetime of a drier is four years.
- Paper towels cost five cents each. The number of paper towels that you need correlates directly with the number of customers you anticipate. So if you expect 50 customers a night, expect they will use 50 towels.
- Toweling rolls cost $5 per roll (and again, you need two—one for each restroom). The rolls are changed daily if there are more than 2,000 customers per month. They are changed every other day if there are less than 2,000 customers per month.

At this point, you know the option you select varies with the number of customers. Therefore, it makes sense to look at a break-even calculation. First of all, take the dryers. They cost $100 per month to operate, plus an upfront charge of $1,000 that depreciates over their lifetime (i.e., an additional $1,000/(4 x 12) per month = $21 per month). Therefore, their total cost is approximately $120 per month, which does not vary with the number of customers coming into the restaurant.

Secondly, look at the paper towels option. These vary directly with number of customers in the restaurant, at a cost of $0.05 per customer. Therefore, assuming few customers per month, paper towels are cheaper than dryers. Figure out how many customers have to come to the restaurant each month to make the dryers more cost effective. The cost of towels would have to exceed $120 per month, equating to 2,400 customers per month ($120/$0.05).

Determine if the rolls option affects this break-even amount. At less than 2,000 customers per month, the rolls cost $10 every other day or $150 per month ($10 x 15 days). This, in itself, costs more than both the dryer and the towels option. With more than 2,000 customers, it only looks less favorable. Therefore, the real economic decision is between towels and dryers. At less than 2,400 customers per month (or 2,400/30 = 80 customers per night), you prefer the towels. Once the number of customers increases above this, you recommend switching to dryers.

Following the economic analysis, drop a few non-economic questions that might sway the balance:

- Are there additional staff costs of cleaning up paper towel waste?
- How many suppliers of each option are there? If there is a single supplier, does he have the power to raise prices in the future?

Guesstimates

In guesstimates, your interviewer generally asks you to estimate the market size for a product or service and observes your reasoning process. The key is not necessarily to get the right answer, but to show your ability to tackle a problem logically, approach assumptions sensibly and perform simple calculations quickly without a calculator.

Guesstimate cracking tips

- For use in your analysis, assume the United States has 270 million people and 25 million businesses. (Consider rounding up to 300 million, as long as you inform your interviewer that you are doing so.)

- Make reasonable assumptions, with rounded, easy-to-work-with numbers (difficult numbers might throw off your calculations), and go from there.

- Remember that you are expected to use a pen and notepad to work through your calculations.

- If you don't know a number, like the population of Brazil or the circumference of the globe, ask for it. Avoid stumbling your way through an answer based on inaccurate assumptions.

- Talk through your steps aloud as you go through your calculations.

- Remember that guesstimates, like cases, also involve elements of creativity and problem solving. For example, when asked "How much change would you find on the floor of a mall?" ask, "Is there a fountain in the mall?"

Sample Guesstimate

1. How many gallons of white paint are sold in the U.S. each year?

The "start big" approach

If unsure where to begin your analysis, start with the basic assumption that 300 million people live in the United States. If 300 million people live in the United States, perhaps half of them live in houses (or 150 million people). The average family size is about three, which measures out to 50 million houses in the United States. Add another 10 percent or so for second houses and houses used for other purposes besides residential. Conclude that there are about 55 million houses.

If houses are painted every 10 years on average, then roughly 5.5 million houses get painted every year. Assuming one gallon covers 100 square feet of wall and the average house has 2,000 square feet, each house needs 20 gallons. Therefore, 110 million gallons of paint are sold per year (five million houses times 20 gallons). (Note: If you want to be clever, ask your interviewer whether to include inner walls as well.) If 80 percent of all houses are white, then 88 million gallons of white house paint are sold each year. (Remember that last step!)

The "start small" approach

Take a town of 30,000 (about 1/10,000th of the population). If you use the same assumption that half the town lives in houses in groups of three, then there are 5,000 houses. Add another 10 percent for good measure, and there are really 5,500 houses in your guesstimate. Painted every 10 years, 550 houses get painted in any given year. If each house has 2,000 square feet of wall, and each gallon covers 100 square feet, then each house needs 20 gallons. Therefore, 11,000 gallons of house paint are sold each year in your typical town. Perhaps 80 percent or 8,800 of those are white. Multiply by 10,000, and you have 88 million gallons.

If your interviewer asks you how you would actually get that number as a consultant, use your creativity—e.g., contact major paint producers, call HUD's statistics arm or conduct a small sample of the second calculation in a few representative towns.

More Sample Guesstimates

1. How many 747s are above Kansas right now?

2. How much beer is consumed in the United States each year?

3. How many barbers are there in Chicago?

4. How many gas stations are there in Los Angeles?

5. What is the annual size of the golf ball market in the United States? What factors drive demand?

6. How many pay phones are there on the island of Manhattan?

Brainteasers

Brainteasers—or, as one disgruntled interviewee referred to them, "mind splitters"—are the genre of questions along the line of, "Why are manhole covers round?" Some brainteasers look more like logic problems, while others require more mathematics. Be forewarned—some of these questions are tricky, and it is possible you might not solve them in a short amount of time. Their main function is to test your courage under fire.

Keep your composure! Do not tell your interviewer that the brainteaser cannot be solved or is unreasonable. As a consultant, you will find yourself on the spot all the time, so your interviewer wants to ensure that you can keep your cool.

Sample Brainteasers

1. You and a neighbor plan garage sales for the same day. You both plan to sell the same used TV model. You want to sell the TV for $100, but your neighbor insists on selling his for $40. What should you do?

Naturally, you think the right answer hinges on compromise—you sell your TV for more than $40 but something less than $100. But in the land of business, the right answer requires taking an underutilized asset and turning it around for profit maximization. In this case, buy your neighbor's TV for $40 and then sell each TV for $100.

2. You stand in a room with three light switches. Each controls one of three light bulbs in the next room. You must figure out which switch controls which bulb. You have some limitations—you can flick only two switches and you may enter the room only once.

Consultants and clients alike love "out-of-the-box" thinking. Some suggest drilling a hole in the wall or calling a friend for assistance. One applicant suggested the switches might be dimmer switches—each light bulb could be set to a certain level of illumination, making solving the puzzle easy. One elegant solution, however, is to turn one light bulb on for 10 minutes and turn it off. Turn another bulb on and go into the room. The light bulb that is on clearly goes with the switch that you turned on last. Now feel the bulbs. The hot one was on recently.

3. Four men must cross a bridge in 17 minutes. The bridge is very narrow and only two men can cross at once. It is nighttime, and whoever is crossing the bridge must carry a flashlight. Alan can cross in one minute, Bert in two, Cedric in five minutes, and Don in 10 minutes. The men crossing the bridge go at the pace of the slowest individual. How should they cross?

First, Alan and Bert cross together with the flashlight, which takes two minutes. Alan returns with the flashlight, which takes one minute. Three minutes have elapsed. Cedric and Don then cross with the flashlight, which takes 10 minutes. At the 13-minute mark, Bert returns with the flashlight, taking two minutes. Bert and Alan go back across the bridge, for a total time elapsed of 17 minutes.

4. Why is a manhole cover round? (The classic brainteaser: Originally asked by Microsoft, this still makes the rounds among consulting and high-tech firms.)

There are many answers to this puzzler. A round manhole cover will not fall into a hole, making it safer. A round manhole cover can be rolled on its edge and will not cut anyone. Round covers also do not need to be rotated to fit over a hole.

Practicing with Your Friends Before the Interview

Practice makes perfect

It is one thing to tear apart a business problem in the privacy of your own space. But it is an entirely different endeavor to walk through that analysis out loud for a complete stranger—someone who has done the analysis herself in the real world, someone who is prepared to challenge your thoughts and even be a bit antagonistic. How many of us have tried to explain a solution to someone else and stumbled on words, stuttered, threw in a few too many ums, or had to retrace our steps after losing our place? How to ensure that you are as eloquent as possible in the interview? Simple: Practice makes perfect.

Smart candidates realize that the case interview is a fit interview in disguise. The interviewer is checking you for analytic aptitude. In addition, the interviewer is getting a sense of what it would be like to work with you. How good are you at communicating your logic? How would clients perceive you? What would you be like to work with on a team? It is just as important to practice the actual vocal delivery of the analysis as it is to be able to think through the analysis itself. Don't forget to smile once in a while!

We know of a handful of people who walked right into their first case interview and nailed it. But for most of us, the case interview can be a tougher communication proposition than public speaking. The better prepared you are to walk through your thinking aloud and explain your analysis in clear, succinct sentences, the better you will do at the real thing.

The good news is that you can learn to crack cases. The best way? Practice. Pair up with your friends, colleagues or classmates. Have one person play the interviewer and the other person play the interviewee. The interviewer should read one of the sample cases beforehand, understand the analysis and be prepared to guide the interviewee through the case. Make sure the interviewee hasn't read through the case ahead of time. The interviewer should then guide the interviewee through a mock interview. At the undergraduate level, include brainteasers and guesstimate questions in addition to a qualitative case. At the MBA level, you will want to use a slightly more complex business case.

After the questions, the interviewer might want to give the interviewee balanced feedback on his or her performance and go over the study notes. For example, you can score the interviewee's performance as follows:

- **Presentation**—Shook hands, smiled, was well-dressed and displayed solid manners and business etiquette throughout. Maintained eye contact throughout the interview. (10 points)

- **Communication**—Relayed thoughts and ideas to the interviewer clearly and succinctly. Explained thought processes in sufficient detail for the interviewer. (30 points)

- **Quantitative Skills**—Showed good facility with numbers, including guesstimates. (15 points)

- **Problem Solving**—Followed a logical, thorough, well-connected path of reasoning to solve the answer. Laid out a road map upfront and continued to think out loud. Used a framework if appropriate. Showed the ability to be flexible and change directions if the interviewer wanted to guide the case a different way. (30 points)

- **Summary**—Wrapped up the case for the interviewer, bringing together the pieces of the puzzle and offering thoughtful recommendations and follow-up insights. (10)

- **Questions**—Asked the interviewer two or three thoughtful questions specific to the interviewer's firm. (5 points)

Of course, the actual breakdown will vary according to each firm you interview with. What will not change is the importance of how well you answer the questions, present yourself and communicate your answer.

Best practices for practicing

Here are a few pointers to make sure you get the most out of your practice sessions.

1. Take it seriously.

If you are the interviewee, bring your leather notepad and favorite pen. Review the frameworks in this guide and apply them judiciously. Don't forget to take notes while the interviewer is speaking, and nod and paraphrase to demonstrate good listening. Above all, don't forget to answer the question.

If you are the interviewer, be realistic. Don't be overly willing to give up the answers or hints without being asked, but if the interviewee asks for some help, go ahead and give it.

2. Simulate the actual case interview format.

Here is the typical format for a case interview (this will, of course, vary depending on the firm):

(1) Direct fit or behavioral questions: Why consulting? Why this firm? Why you? (5-10 minutes)

(2) Case questions (15-20 minutes)

(3) Questions for the interviewer (3-5 minutes)

Case interviews often start with a handful of behavioral interview questions, and almost all of the time they will fall in some form of the three basic questions in (1). The interviewee should have quick, thorough answers to these questions ready. Also, pretend the interviewer is from a specific consulting firm, and have the interviewee prepare a few questions to ask the interviewer at the end.

3. Focus on communication.

This is a great environment for the interviewee to practice communicating his or her analysis in a succinct, clear, engaging manner.

4. Practice with different types of people.

You never know what kind of personality your interviewer will have, and you don't want to get used to a certain case giver's style. Moreover, we tend to be a little more forgiving of our friends. Try practicing with people you don't know very well but who are willing to help you. These include current consultants, alumni of your school, career services employees or fellow students.

Questions for the Interviewer

Every single consulting interview ends with an opportunity for the candidate to ask the interviewer a few questions about the firm. Some candidates come unprepared for this and have nothing to ask. Arrive prepared to ask a few questions of your interviewer.

Remember, you are evaluating the firm as well. What would you need to know in order to make your decision? Would you need to hear an honest answer about the travel load? Are you concerned about the firm's early requirement of industry specialization? Before your interview, take a few minutes and think through what key questions you must have answered. If you won't work anywhere that won't let you transfer to the San Francisco office in two years, you'd better ask!

Interview Questions that Never Get Asked (But Are Always Answered)

At its heart, consulting is a business about people. Hiring consultants will look for anything that resembles poor personal skills in the screening process. We know far too many anecdotes of folks with great consulting skills shooting themselves in the foot by not taking care of the basics, such as grooming and etiquette.

In addition to the usual interview questions, consultants are looking to answer three implicit questions about each of the people they interview. Make sure you give your interviewer the right answers to these questions.

- **Does this person really want to work here?** Does he or she seem genuinely enthusiastic about the consulting industry and, specifically, this firm? Did this person care enough to look the part or did he/she just slap on a suit and run out the door? Did this person show up on time? Did this person ask thoughtful questions at the end of the interview?

- **Could I put this person in front of the client?** The interviewer is assessing your professionalism. He or she wants to find out if you would be a solid representative of the firm to the client. Your speech is especially important; if you are too nervous or not eloquent, the interviewer may doubt your ability to run or participate in a meeting or interview.

- **Would I want to work with this person?** Recall the "airplane test." The interviewer wants to hire someone likeable, someone with whom he or she could work late into the night, wait in an airport, drive to the client or share a meal. A decent sense of humor and the all-important spark of energy should be there as well. In other words, the interviewer is deciding if he or she would want you on the same project team.

How does an interviewer answer these questions? The following sections cover aspects of the interview that help answer them. These issues may seem so fundamental that attention need not be paid to them, but in some ways these presentation elements are the most important aspects of your consulting interview.

Dress the part

There's no reason to max out your credit cards on the swankiest of Armani suits. Still, presentation is important. It speaks to your interest in the firm and the impression you will make on clients.

How should you dress for interviews? Even though consultants are shifting to business casual in the office and on client sites, interview protocol hasn't changed that much. Unless specifically told otherwise, stick with business formal in the interview. Men should wear a pressed dark suit, clean shirt, tie, belt, dark socks, and polished dark shoes. (Bonus points for those gentlemen who successfully match the belt with the shoes.) Women should wear a dark suit (either pants or skirt), a blouse or coordinating crew-neck sweater, stockings, and nice shoes (either heels or pumps). Dress as if you are already a consultant with the firm.

Look yourself over before you head out the door and make sure you don't have any "negative distractions." These include things like ripped stockings and untied shoes. One candidate was an Ivy League honors student with great leadership experience and terrific problem-solving skills. He interviewed with a leading IT consultancy and had a great interview; the interviewer was visibly impressed that he had nailed the case, and the two had good rapport. Smiling, the young man went home, stopped in the bathroom, and was horrified to see that one of the two buttons on his shirt collar was unattached. It was a small thing, but it looked very sloppy. The message on his answering machine the next day informed him that he wouldn't be called back for the second round. While he never confirmed if the shirt collar did him in, he wonders to this day if that was the reason he didn't make it. Again, it's about reflecting that you cared enough to take care of the easy details. (On some level, the interviewer might extrapolate such details to how careful you would be with your Excel spreadsheet.)

What to bring

We mentioned before that you should bring a pad and a reliable pen. Another companion for consulting interviews should be a leather or high-quality vinyl portfolio that holds a single letter-sized notepad. Here's what you should put in it:

- **Clean pad of paper**—It doesn't have to be graph paper, but it should be something you feel comfortable working out problems on.

- **Pen or pencil**—Test it out beforehand! The horror stories about interviewees asking their interviewer for a pen exist for a reason. Remember that you will likely be using this device for note taking and calculations, so bring your favorite instrument. And bring a spare.

- **A few extra copies of your resume**—Your interviewer will likely have a copy already, but it never hurts to have some handy, especially if you have updates.

- **Some notes on the company**—You will probably have a few minutes before your interview to review your thoughts, so jot down the key points and a couple of burning questions neatly on a piece of paper and stick it in your folder.

Try to take only the bare minimum into the interview room. Leave your attaché in the hall closet of the firm or recruiting center; women typically bring their purse to the interview.

Behavior

There are some time-tested best practices for conducting oneself in a stressful environment like a consulting interview.

- **Firm handshake**—It isn't that the firm handshake necessarily enhances one's impression of another; it's that a weak handshake usually causes a negative impression. Don't try to crack your interviewer's knuckles or anything, just make sure you have a nice and solid grip. Wipe those sweaty palms on a handkerchief before you go in.

- **Maintain eye contact**—Try not to look down as you speak, and, except for when you need to write or glance at your notes, keep your head high and speak to the interviewer. Think of the interview as a conversation, not a test.

- **Speak slowly**—When people are nervous, they tend to speak faster. The result is that your interviewer will think you are less articulate than you really are and worry about your cool under pressure. Try to be aware of your overall tempo. If you finding yourself rushing, just relax, take a deep breath and slow down. Take 10 seconds if you need to, or sip some water to stall. Here's another slowdown tactic: When you need to pause, instead of using "um," say the word "now," as in "now…looking at the company's costs…" You'll find this works as a natural break in the action without losing the overall flow.

- **Keep out the distractions**—Try to avoid little movements and gestures that divert the interviewer's attention from the content of the interview. Examples include constantly brushing your hair out of your eyes, checking a clock or your watch, fidgeting, itching or playing with your pen. We all do these things; in the interview context, they reflect insecurity. When you practice your interviews with others, ask for their feedback on the little distractions. You can also set yourself up for success by tying your hair back and keeping your watch at home.

- **Be good-natured and energetic**—Smile. Don't slouch. Don't touch your face. Speak passionately about the things that matter to you and stay optimistic. If you get a bizarre question, laugh it off and do your best. After all, it's just an interview!

- **Ask for feedback**—After your interview, if you think you've had good rapport with your interviewer, ask for a 10-second summary of your strengths and weaknesses. Consultants must be willing to ask for, and accept feedback. Your proactive approach will work in your favor. At the very least, it will help you with future interviews.

Post-Interview: Accepting, Negotiating, Declining

CHAPTER 6

After the Interview

Whew! Wait until you walk out of the firm's elevator bank or your school's career center; then you can at last take a deep breath, relax and enjoy the rest of the day. Then, start thinking about the next steps in the interview process.

Confirm next steps

If you just finished an interview round on campus, you probably already know the next steps (the firm's recruiter will call you Thursday, you will get an e-mail with the results, etc.). If you interviewed outside of the school's official recruiting cycles, or if you just finished final round interviews at the firm's office downtown, you will want to get some expectation of when you will hear the results. The easiest thing to do is to remember to ask the recruiting manager (likely not one of your interviewers) on the way out the door. If you forget, you can simply send an e-mail or give the recruiting contact a call the next day to confirm.

Thank your interviewers

Good form includes sending a thank-you note to your interviewers. This can be a very short message that thanks the interviewer for his or her time, reminds the person of one or two key items that you discussed, and reiterates why you are sincerely interested in the firm. Mention a couple of discussion points from the interview, because the interviewers speak to so many candidates that they will appreciate the teasers you send to refresh their memory (and will likely make you stand out in their minds).

A letter or thank-you note used to be the way to go, but these days, an e-mail to the interviewer works fine. Send the thank-you note no later than the day after the interview.

Waiting for an offer

Perhaps the most stressful time of the entire process is after all the interviews, waiting to see if you got the job or not. Realize that at this point you've done all you can, and the decision is now fully out of your hands. You might as well enjoy the fact that you don't have to worry about this firm for a little while.

So what do you do when the agreed-upon day of reckoning comes, and there's no phone call? This will happen from time to time. Be patient. Wait a day, then call your recruiting contact to find out where you stand. A call works better than an e-mail, because it is more personal and reminds the firm that you are waiting on pins and needles.

If you are going through on-campus recruiting and do not receive the answer within three to five business days of the date you were given for the firm's reply deadline, notify your career services office. The career office acts as your agent and enforces guidelines for the firms.

Accepting an Offer

One of the firm's partners has called to extend you an offer to join the firm. In a few days, you will formally receive the offer in writing. Congratulations! This is exactly what you've been working toward, and now you've got it.

If you've read the offer letter word by word and you are pleased with the package, you have the delightful job of informing the firm that you wish to accept the offer. Telling the firm "yes" is the fun and easy part. There are three steps. Leave a phone message with the recruiting manager, so they know to expect your paperwork in the mail. Sign and photocopy all of the documents. Send in the paperwork. That's it!

We recommend that you don't turn down other offers until you have formally accepted another. Also, do not consider a verbal offer a real offer—wait until you get it in writing.

If you've negotiated any additional points in your offer letter, be sure that you've captured them in an e-mail at the very least. Getting items in writing on the firm's letterhead is better. You may need to refer to them later.

Negotiating an Offer

Many candidates wish to negotiate the terms of their offer. Be warned that the extent to which you can negotiate the terms of your offer depends highly on the balance of power in the job market. In the late 1990s, the job market was an employee's market: Corporate growth was all the rage and companies would add extra benefits like a few thousand more dollars on the signing bonus or an extra week of vacation to get employees in the door. In the early years of the current decade, it has been a recruiter's market: New jobs are few and far between, and the lucky candidates with job offers are being given lower compensation and fewer benefits, with little room for negotiation.

That said, there are some time-tested best practices for negotiating parts of consulting offers. No matter how the economy's doing, it is always worth a try. Just make sure you're pleasant and businesslike.

Office location

Changing locations after the offer is given is tough. Unless you have a compelling reason for the switch, you may find it difficult to change offices. Your chances are better if you're trying to switch from a more desirable office to an understaffed office.

Whatever the reason, first try explaining the reason for your office change to your recruiting manager and ask that person to look into the switch. They will either tell you no off the bat or look into the transfer. If the person agrees to look into the matter, make sure you both commit to a later date to follow up.

What if your request is turned down? Don't quit there. See if you can find someone in the target office to vouch for the office transfer—the higher up (partner or senior manager), the better. When you have found the person, explain your situation, describe why you really want to be a part of that person's office community and ask if there's anything he or she can do. Offer to fly out to the office and meet with the consultants there in person. (If they agree to this, your trip will be worth the money.) This is obviously a different angle to pursue, but it's worth a shot. Along the way, try to gauge whether or not you seem "needy" or "difficult" and scale back your efforts accordingly—you'd hate to start off on the wrong foot with this company.

Start date

It's usually difficult to get an employer to start you earlier than your given start date. Sometimes if the firm is sold out, the firm will gladly bring you on a month or two earlier. On the other hand, it's usually the case that the firm has carefully timed your start date to their expected project pipeline, and if anything, you would likely be able to negotiate a later start date. The key selling point from your end is that the firm could start paying your salary later than they had planned, which would save the firm money.

Salary and bonus

Getting more money is always tough, especially in a recruiter's market, so don't expect to be able to improve your compensation package. (Just be glad you have one!) The best point of leverage would be to have another job offer in hand that offers more money. You can tell your firm contacts, "I really like your firm best; however, I have to admit that this competing offer is compelling because the salary is $10,000 higher. I'm ready to sign with you if we can make my numbers better. What can you do to improve my compensation package?" If you are an MBA or a lateral hire, you might have another point of negotiation if your previous salary was higher, because then you might be able to convince the employer that you are being undervalued. Do not under any circumstances invent a fake job offer for negotiating leverage.

Starting position

An MBA with prior consulting experience or a lateral hire might be given a first-year associate offer. If you are one of these people, and you feel like you are starting at a lower level than you should be, ask for a shorter initial review cycle, such as after six months instead of one year. This gives you a chance to prove your worth. At larger firms this isn't easy because there are so many other new hires at your level and it's hard to make exceptions; smaller firms might be willing to be more flexible.

If you can successfully negotiate for a shorter review period, don't forget to get it in writing; it would be easy for the firm to let this slip through the cracks.

Vacation

If you don't like the vacation package and the firm won't grant you any more vacation days, ask about the firm's unpaid leave policy. If the firm doesn't have one, get written confirmation (e-mail is fine) that you would be able to take extra days of unpaid vacation. There is no reason why a firm shouldn't be willing to withhold pay for a few days per year. A lot of firms offer discretionary time off along these lines.

Offer response deadline

Your offer letter will usually have a date listed, stating when you should let HR know if you're coming onboard or not. Don't forget to ask for a deadline extension if you need it—surprisingly, this often turns out to be negotiable. It's a very common thing to get a little more time to make a decision, so don't feel weird about asking for it.

Turning Down an Offer

You may be one of those lucky people with more than one consulting offer, which means that you will have to turn down one or more of them. The goal is to turn down the offer in such a way that you stand the best chance of preserving your relationship with the firm.

A prime example of the importance of relationship management involves a 2006 graduate of a top-five MBA program named Rick. Rick was deciding between two equally compelling job offers from top consultancies, Firm 1 and Firm 2. Rick chose Firm 1 over Firm 2, based on a higher pay package (a difference of $50,000) and a location that would keep him closer to his wife. When Rick conveyed his decline of the offer to Firm 2, he stressed the fact that he really wanted to work at Firm 2 (which was entirely true), that the location was the deciding factor and that he really wanted to make the relationship with Firm 2 work. Firm 2 understood, and told him that if he could indeed get the location to work out, Rick would be always welcome to join Firm 2 if it had a job for him.

As luck (bad luck, in this case) would have it, Firm 1 soon delayed Rick's start date indefinitely due to financial problems. Rick immediately called up Firm 2, explained the situation, and offered to move to a different location away from his wife. Firm 2 said it was not in a strong enough economic position to reextend the offer, but invited Rick to keep in touch. Once a month, Rick called his contacts at Firm 2 to remind them that he was still available. Each time, Firm 2 said it still was not in a position to hire him. Nine months later, Firm 2 called Rick, informed him that it was looking to staff up, and because of his efforts to stay in touch, was prepared to offer him a position with the firm. He accepted, and he and his wife moved to the city where Firm 2 was headquartered. He still works with Firm 2 to this day. Meanwhile, Firm 1 never offered Rick a start date.

This is a true story of outstanding relationship management, and in today's difficult employment environment we encourage you to manage all of your relationships this well. We suggest a few guidelines for declining an offer and preserving your relationship with that firm.

- **Comply with the deadlines**—Even if you must decline an offer, tell the firm of your decision by the appropriate deadline.
- **Call instead of e-mailing**—E-mail is still a relatively impersonal form of communication. Remember that you are communicating a rejection to someone else. A team of partners sat around a table, thought hard and decided to bring you into their firm. You should follow up with a note or e-mail.
- **Be polite**—Be straightforward and even mildly apologetic when you break the news. Express your gratitude for the offer.
- **Try to frame your reason as external**—The firm will likely ask you for a reason why you choose not to work with them. Present the reason that seems the least personal. Suppose, for example, that you choose ABC over XYZ was for two reasons—you found XYZ's people to be nice but slightly aloof, and because XYZ's offer was for Boston and ABC's offer was for Denver, where your parents live. You might offer the following as a reason for not choosing XYZ: "I really wanted to work at XYZ, but in the end I needed to be closer to my family in Denver. I hope to make the relationship with XYZ work in the future." This approach will help preserve your relationship with XYZ.

Again, before you turn down any offers in favor of another, wait until you have accepted the other offer and received confirmation.

What to Do When Things Don't Work Out

Dealing with rejection (and overcoming it)

If you don't get an offer after the interview, don't take it personally. Remember that literally thousands of people must have applied for the job you did, and most of them didn't even get interviews.

First, make sure that you get feedback on your interview. Seek to understand what you did well and what areas you can improve. Most firms will volunteer this information. If you didn't receive feedback, ask for it.

You also want to find out when you might apply again. Do you need to wait until the next fall? Or, if you work a different job in the meantime, could you get hired off-cycle as a lateral hire? Find out when to get in touch (if you are still interested in working with the firm) and whom to contact. There's an unwritten rule that you have to wait a full two years before reapplying to a firm, but obviously it varies company to company.

If it sounds like you were close to an offer, and you can identify the decision makers, you may want to make the following suggestions to still get your foot in the door.

- **Project employment**—Acknowledge that the firm has doubts about you. State that you are committed to the firm. Suggest that you work with the firm on one project only. Point out that this gives the firm help on projects, yet binds them in no way. You can further sweeten the deal for the firm by confirming that you wouldn't need benefits as a contractor.

- **Work for free**—This is the way to get experience under your belt if you have no other offers. Simply offer your services without pay on a per-project basis. Part-time work may also be effective.

- **Backup materials**—What do they have doubts about? If it's your writing ability, send them a sample. If it's smarts, e-mail some backup scores or a letter of reference. Perhaps you can change their perception of you.

Obviously, it is very difficult to overcome a denial of an offer, but we know folks for whom these strategies have worked. It may work for you.

Dealing with rescinded offers

Those who attempted to earn consulting job offers in the early 2000s know that a germane, unfortunate consequence of a weak economy is that many consulting firms, realizing that they have overhired given their projected project pipeline, wind up rescinding or delaying job offers they've given out. This is obviously very disruptive to those prospective consultants who practiced hard for their case interviews, only to have their job offers evaporate or recede into the hazy future. You may find yourself reading this and being shocked that this practice ever happens—isn't it illegal? It's not. Job offers have fine print buried in them that inform you that either you or the firm could, at any time and without any good reason, terminate that offer. It's hard to believe in this day and age of robust job offers, so consider yourself forewarned.

- **If a firm rescinds its offer to you, try to understand what this means.** Will they never honor the offer? Have they rescinded all offers? What is the procedure for getting rehired, if any? Would you get any special consideration in the next go-around, given how unfairly you have been treated and how you turned down other offers in favor of the promises made by their firm? In compensation for lost income at the rescinding firms and the missed income from offers you turned down, what severance package will you get? Understand what the true impact is on you and what benefits you might get.

- **Attempt to negotiate a delayed start date instead of a rescinded offer.** A delayed start would mean that when the economy picks up and the firm can make good on its offers, you will be hired first because you've already passed the screening process. In other words, you are saving them money.

- **If you can't get a delayed start date, push for a severance package.** Firms should offer you something.

- **Rescinded offers are taboo on campus.** Several business schools (such as Harvard and Wharton) will put firms on probation for a set period of time, should they rescind offers. If you're on campus, tell your career services center so they can take appropriate actions.

- **Now is the time to tap into your network for other opportunities.** If you turned down other offers, start with those firms, as well as any firms you interviewed with but didn't get offers from. Offer options in the vein of those we listed in the previous section.

- In all likelihood, you are stuck with restarting the recruiting cycle. However, be encouraged by the fact that you are no doubt in good company with the others in the same boat.

You might feel like your world is collapsing in on you if your offer is rescinded. Take a deep breath. Understand what it means, tap into your network, and remember that things will work out.

Dealing with delayed offers

As we mentioned before, in a difficult economic climate, firms may offer new hires a delayed start date, also known as a deferral. As of publication of this guide, such developments are nowhere on the horizon, but you never know what may happen in the volatile world of consulting.

A deferral is a rather creative way for HR departments to help manage labor costs. Firms simply inform their new hires that they will have to delay their start date, and often offer the new hires the chance to walk away or wait for the start date to kick in. In some cases, firms have offered new hires cash to continue waiting; in others, firms have offered cash equivalents (like the keeping of a signing bonus) for new hires to walk away and exit the firm's job pipeline. In effect, the employment offer turns into an option on future employees. (For example, back in 2001, firms such as McKinsey, Accenture and Booz Allen Hamilton deferred almost all of their new hires, and ultimately rescinded offers to many of them).

As a deferred new hire, what can you do? You can attempt to accelerate your hiring process. This is obviously difficult, but there are things you can try. Call up the partner who hired you or any other senior person you know, explain your situation (they might not even know about it) and ask if you could work on a per-project or part-time basis with them. Many firms have an infrastructure to bring on cheap labor like outside consultants—why not you, since you've been prescreened? If your contact doesn't require your help, push to see if he or she will circulate your resume to colleagues. If you can somehow get into the system, you might be able to get hired more quickly. Confirm who your official firm contact is, and stay on that person's radar. Call them up monthly to get an update, even if there's nothing to report. Strive to be first in that person's mind should an interim opportunity arise.

If you have no other job options, you should stay in the pipeline, because eventually (though who knows when) you will have a job at that company.

There is absolutely no point in stepping out of the pipeline—why destroy a future option for yourself?

At the same time, continue your job search. The problem with being deferred is that you feel like you're in limbo. This could prevent you from entering a full-fledged job search. The fact is, if you've been deferred, you currently have no job. Please don't fall into the trap of thinking that you do.

Hit up your network of job contacts (again, anywhere you have an "in," especially offers you've turned down and firms where you got an interview) and start the cycle again.

In the interim, you will have some downtime. Keep your brain sharp by studying and reading. See if you can help out your favorite professors from college or business school with research or their own consulting gigs.

Finally, don't forget to stay in touch with your friends and family—use this opportunity to make sure your emotional "bank account" is full.

ON THE JOB

Chapter 7: The Project Life Cycle

Chapter 8: Tips for High Performance

Chapter 9: The Consulting Career Path

Chapter 10: Our Survey Says: The Consulting Lifestyle

Chapter 11: Days in the Life

The Project Life Cycle

CHAPTER 7

The Project Life Cycle

Pitching/proposal/letter of engagement

Compared to investment bankers, management consultants spend comparatively little time in a formal pitching process. Partners carry out the main pitch process. They either respond to the initial approach of current or potential clients, or they identify new or follow-up studies with past clients. Sometimes companies will issue a Request for Proposal (RFP) to solicit bids for consultants for a specific purpose; consulting firms often seek out RFP opportunities and respond to the relevant ones immediately. Associates generally get involved in some initial non-billable work (research, mainly) to support the partners' conversations with the client.

To do more than support the initial conversations, do your part to land new clients and engagements. Research the industry for new studies your firm would want to publish. Approach past clients for organizational pulse checks. When at a client, keep your eyes and ears open for new opportunities. Tap your alumni network effectively—surf your company's online directory for alums that are senior managers in your target industries and get advice from partners in your firm on leveraging that point of contact. By taking these steps, you become more visible and might even receive a nice bonus check, raise or promotion for all your efforts.

The ultimate aim of the pitch process is the drafting of a proposal. The proposal lays out how and on what the consulting team will focus their efforts, and what results the client should expect. Proposals also detail consulting and client resources and expected length of the engagement. And they might or might not touch upon the sensitive topic of remuneration. Proposals can be in either Word or PowerPoint format.

You might think proposals sound dry and boring, but in consulting they aren't. If you're truly into consulting, you should feel pumped at the notion of putting on paper at a high level what a company needs to improve its business. It doesn't get closer to the core of the business than that.

Sometimes, after the proposal, there's a separate document called the "letter of engagement." This might be the same thing as a Word-based proposal document. The common difference is that the proposal could be a higher-level detailed framing document that the client agrees to in principal, whereas the letter of engagement gets into more details about the project elements, timeline, staff and professional fees. Different firms handle it different ways, and sometimes it varies within a firm, too.

We recommend you try to get involved in the engagement at the early stage of sales if you can. First, it provides a good chance to get up to speed on the client and industry before the study starts in earnest. Second, you might mitigate a partner's optimistic estimates of the team's performance efficiency and make yourself a hero in the end. Finally, it will give you a window into the guts of consulting (strategic selling) and inform your understanding of whether you want to be in this job for the long haul (because someday you'll be running such a sales process if you stick it out enough).

Brainstorming/hypothesis generation

With the proposal and/or letter of engagement signed by the client, the project starts. The first few days are normally spent in an intensive round of brainstorming involving the full consulting team and sometimes client members. The team digs into the details, generates a spectrum of options to investigate and narrows these down to a few hypotheses. This approach, used by most major consulting firms, limits the data gathering and analysis to prevent considering an overly broad range of data. (The contrasting approach to "hypothesis-driven analysis" is called "data-driven analysis," which involves gathering most of the available data out there and synthesizing it into what matters and what doesn't. This is a perfectly fine approach, but you don't always have time to do this. As an extreme example, imagine if your doctor used data-driven analysis instead of hypothesis-driven analysis!)

Brainstorming can be both the most exciting and the most frustrating stage of the project. On the one hand, a new consultant sees firsthand how more senior team members tackle the problem set before them. On the other hand, the team might not seem to be making much headway. Ideas are tossed about without any data backing them up. Sensitive egos get bruised because some ideas are rejected. But effective communication (which includes the underestimated power of listening well) during these sessions will guarantee you brainstorming success.

The final part of brainstorming takes each emerging hypothesis and determines how to prove or disprove it in the analysis stage. The team creates a course of action for each case by deciding:

- What data will be required?

- How will it be gathered?
- Who will take responsibility for each part of the analysis?
- How will results be presented?
- How will issues be determined and resolved?
- What information will carry the most weight?

Data gathering and analysis

The meat of the engagement is the data gathering and analysis phase. Although the hypothesis helps focus the task, data gathering can still be overwhelming. (Many consultants fear "boiling the ocean" at this stage—considering an impossibly large amount of data.) Your initial port of call is likely an Internet search—use your favorite search engine to do an initial pull of articles and data sources. (It's therefore important that you learn how to use an Internet search engine's syntax effectively.) If you are in a fairly large consulting firm, leverage your in-house consulting library of books, articles and prior consulting project work. The next option is asking the client for pertinent information—both of which tend to result in large stacks of articles, brokers' and annual reports and other reference materials. Finally, you can identify experts or consultants from your firm who hold similar but nonconflicting projects in their portfolios.

During this stage, you tap internal sources of information provided by the client, from systems and databases to extensive interviews with client personnel. Some studies require you to consult industry experts for their experience, while others necessitate more hands-on measures. Hands-on measures can be critical, but tend not to be so glamorous. Some real-life examples include sitting outside a competitor's factory to count in- and outgoing trucks over several days and taking an inventory of an ice cream company's flavors from inside huge freezers.

However the data is collected, there will be plenty of it—but remember that little of the data will exactly prove or disprove your point, and not all of the data will be relevant. This is where a consultant's ingenuity comes to bear: re-cutting data, combining data sources and making judicious assumptions to support or negate the hypothesis you are trying to test. (Just be sure your clients and your management sign off on your assumptions before proceeding!)

Pulling out conclusions and building the story

Developing a story is an evolving process throughout the project, and it starts at hypothesis generation. As a forcing mechanism, many consultants draft a flexible final presentation at this stage, based on their emerging hypotheses. The team integrates new analysis into the overall puzzle, notes the ripple effects and revises the analysis to take the changes into account. By developing the storyboard first, the team must take a 50,000 foot view and ensure they answer the client's key questions directly. Some consulting firms like to start with one story and map out many endings to see which ones are most effective. The project manager and sometimes the partner, who have been less in the weeds of the project from the get-go, are usually best positioned to take on the initial cut of the storyboard, with the consultants and analysts filling in the pieces.

If you have the opportunity to work on a storyboard, take it. This part of the project has extremely high value add, and you really assemble the reasons you're on the engagement in the first place by pulling together what is relevant for the client. It's also one of the more challenging pieces of the project when it comes up, but it'll test you in a way that you'll find very rewarding later.

Presentation to client

How frequently and in what format the team updates the client varies widely, depending on the engagement. When the client is involved on a day-to-day basis, communication tends to be more frequent and informal. If most of the analysis takes place at the office, client updates might be scheduled on a biweekly or monthly basis. These updates are two-way and critical to the success of the project. During these sessions, the client communicates what its management wants or thinks.

This is also your opportunity to confirm the project's direction and success. "Scope creep"—when clients add additional tasks and expectations to a project—often delays timely success. You must understand how to manage your client's expectations throughout the project, but most especially at these status meetings. However, if your client insists, notify your partners immediately and discuss before you or your manager go to the trouble of creating an addendum to your proposal and having it signed.

Consultants present each finished phase of a project and their major findings to the decision makers owning the project's final recommendation. This "decision board" ranges in level from VP/SVP to C-level, all the way up to the board of directors. Formal presentations are posed as a landscape of exhibits, held together by the aforementioned story line. The partner or director generally runs the meeting. A manager usually owns the final draft of presentation, though this job sometimes falls to an associate who had assumed ownership for part of the project. If the project has been run well, the clients will encounter no major surprises.

If you're on your first project, don't expect that you'll be presenting this time around to the client. You might be asked to, but you would likely feel more comfortable sitting a few reps out and watching how your partner or manager does it. This is not to say that you should decline the opportunity if it comes up; just be realistic about positioning yourself for success so you can feel very good about your first formal client presentation.

Wondering what it's like to work at a specific employer?

Read what EMPLOYEES have to say about:
- Workplace culture
- Compensation
- Hours
- Diversity
- Hiring process

Read employer surveys on THOUSANDS of top employers.

V ULT
> the most trusted name in career information™

Go to www.vault.com

Tips for High Performance
CHAPTER 8

Troubleshooting

Getting personal

Many consultants are fresh out of top schools, smooth operators eager to make their mark in the business world. They may lack industry knowledge or know little about the fundamentals of big business, but they know how to interact with people. No one gets a job offer in consulting without having a penchant for person-to-person interaction. Clients absolutely demand it and consulting firms consider it a prerequisite for the job.

But keep in mind (as we mentioned before) that you don't have to be an extrovert to succeed as a consultant. It's fine to have a preference for introversion. What's vitally important is that the introvert can turn off the preference for solitude when necessary and really work the client relationship through daily interaction and formal presentation. (On the flip side, the overly extroverted personality can be inappropriate in a client setting.)

Consulting firms actively screen candidates for the ability to establish professional relationships, handle pressure and communicate effectively. Consulting interviews, apart from being tools to learn a candidate's background, are meant to test these skills and see how candidates will perform in front of clients. The whole experience is a simulation where the candidate plays the role of consultant, and the firm sits back and judges what it hears. Did you structure your thoughts? Were you comfortable answering complex questions? Were you convincing? (Recall the section "Interview Questions That Never Get Asked (But Are Always Answered)".)

A common mistake for would-be consultants is to concentrate so strongly on acing case questions that they forget to be engaging and personable with their interviewers. Clients want more than long, hyper-logical answers to every question. They also want to make small talk, trade stories and feel as if they are a valuable part of the conversation. (Don't overdo it.) Consulting interviewers are on the lookout for anyone who, despite being extremely intelligent, cannot communicate in a way that makes the client feel involved and appreciated. Those people will not get job offers.

Of course, clients are often twice as demanding and create far greater challenges than anything experienced in consulting interviews. Consulting training, therefore, is geared heavily toward preparing new hires for an ever-demanding professional experience. Being smooth gets you in the door, but it's only a foundation for the advanced skills you will need down the road.

Keep your counsel

One of the first lessons new consultants must learn is the proper care and feeding of clients. It's not uncommon for new hires to be overwhelmed and uncertain at first about how to deal with clients. Clients are often much older than new consultants. It's often unclear who's in charge of consulting projects—the consultant or the client. And it's easy to mistake a good working relationship for a stronger bond.

Experienced consultants, however, have learned how to play by the implicit client-consultant rules. They never forget, first and foremost, that a client is a client, not a buddy. This might seem obvious, but it's not unheard of for consultants to let down their guard during a friendly golf game or a client dinner. Tell your client that his boss is a moron or doesn't care about the engagement, and even if you're right, you shouldn't be surprised to find yourself yanked unceremoniously from the engagement. And neither the client nor your employer will be happy with you. Respect your clients, but don't get too close.

Sell, don't study

For consulting managers and partners, the essence of consulting has little to do with locating a client's problems, identifying solutions or driving large-scale change. Consulting, at its fundamental core, is about completing the terms of relationship, making the client happy and getting a referral for more business. That is, the primary focal point of consulting engagements is selling follow-up engagements. Consulting executives know that all the brilliance in the world doesn't matter unless, at the end of the project, the client is happy. That means if you don't make the client happy, your manager will not be happy with you.

Some consultants have a hard time understanding this. Armed with their Fulbright scholarships, valedictorian plaques or reputations for solving difficult problems at the speed of light, some consultants have difficulty prioritizing interpersonal relations over intellectual achievement. Of course, smarts and creative thinking are essential to the completion of the consultant's tasks. But—and this is a big but—if the project is completed through steamrolling client objections, scoffing at client ideas and otherwise behaving in an arrogant, "I'm-24-and-run-the-company" manner, your client will still be unhappy.

You may not have P&L responsibility for many years, but you should do all you can to support the account leader's efforts to win follow-on sales. The golden rule for you is that the best way to sell follow-on work is to deliver outstanding work. In other words, do your best and the client will ask for more. It sounds simple, and it is.

Your client is not stupid

We now circle back to a point we made at the very beginning of the book, because it's one of the most important ones, and it's probably the easiest to forget as you get caught up in the glamorous, soapbox-standing world that is consulting.

Many consulting engagements are held in the confines of large, corporate headquarters where organizational clarity is, in theory, supposed to exist. Upon arriving at a client site, consultants are often taken aback by the lack of process, frustrated by the poor communication between departments and shocked that no one seems to care. How the hell does this place make money? "I," thinks the new consultant, "could do a better job in two months than the leaders of this place could do in a lifetime."

This sort of arrogance is all too common in consultants. Overconfident consultants think that by observing the client for a while or by reading a brief company history, they will be able to identify and solve every single problem that exists in that company. What they fail to realize is that people on the client team have been working at the company for years, sometimes decades. Their institutional knowledge can be extensive and extremely helpful, and their ability to maneuver through their company's culture can save consultants a lot of heartache. Scoff at your own risk. Clients often know more about their companies than you ever will, so rely on them for occasional help—or drown in your own ignorance.

Be careful in your attitude toward the client. Clients know when consultants do not approve of the job they are doing. And have some sensitivity. It's galling to have all your problems examined openly by strangers—and used as examples of faulty thinking.

Do you still think the client is stupid? Just remember that the client hired you, so how stupid can they be? Also recall that the client signs your checks. The client has the power to support, or not support, every single initiative consultants so brilliantly suggest. Anger the client and you may as well start writing the project's obituary.

Like it or not, the client is central to consulting projects. Consulting may have the allure of being a think-tank experience with no running commentary from outside observers, but that is only half true. The reality is that clients are involved in the process nearly every day, that factions within companies have power (and need to be neutralized) and that right answers, no matter how impressive, are worthless without client buy-in.

Nothing does more to stunt a consultant's learning than this type of attitude. In fact, it is nearly impossible to consult with any effectiveness if the client is stereotyped, underestimated or ignored. Clients hold the keys to mountains of useful information, and they either make this information available or they don't.

Consulting versus body-shopping

Consulting doesn't always involve wining and dining CEOs and offering high-level strategy advice to beleaguered corporations. Sometimes consultants are mere soldiers on the battleground of business, conducting training seminars, crunching numbers in nameless Excel spreadsheets and even making catering arrangements for conferences.

Consulting, traditionally speaking, centers around the client relationship, the exchange of ideas and advice, the large question-answer sessions that lead to corporate breakthroughs, long, raucous client dinners and real, progressive change. This is the dream offered by strategy shops like McKinsey, Bain, Oliver Wyman and the like. But much of what the average consultant actually does involves coding in a hastily-learned spreadsheet language, trying out PowerPoint skills to compile presentations, writing memos and performing other maintenance tasks that almost certainly could be done more cheaply by the client's employees. This is, for lack of a better word, called body-shopping.

Sometimes, consultants may begin an engagement as strategists and end as body shop workers. For many client teams, sticking to original project plans is a very difficult task. Clients often see consultants as a fresh source of labor. If consulting executives don't push back and enforce the original agreement, consultants may end up doing routine tasks. Body-shopping engagements can end badly, with both client and consulting firm trying to figure out why the highly-skilled consultants ended up doing such routine work.

That said, body-shopping is sometimes a good thing because you get to be part of the client organization for a period of time. In an engagement called "Project Backfill," (like the name?) a team of four consultants served as temporary labor for the quantitative analytics department of an energy company. Each consultant led and/or completed several one-off investment analysis projects over a span of six months. In the process, the consultants learned a heck of a lot about the power generation business and worked with some extremely nice engineers and corporate finance analysts. In this case, body-shopping turned out to be a great experience. It all depends on where your client sits in the organization.

How To Survive Your First Month on the Job

Before you walk in the door

What if you were a comparative literature major in college, got the consulting job by studying your case interviews and honestly don't know a lick about the business world? Will you be behind the curve? Will you fail? Should you not have applied in the first place? The answers are all no, but only if you take some preparatory steps before you start work. (Such steps are useful even if you have some business experience).

- **Familiarize yourself with the firm.** Remind yourself about the training programs, office locations, staffing process and other aspects of the company. This is not so you can pass a multiple-choice exam but so you can have some refreshed context when you start your job.

- **Get some advice.** Talk to alums of your school or people in your professional network who have worked there or currently work there. Pick their brains about key dos and don'ts. See what the right recipe for success might be.

- **Educate yourself as necessary.** Pick up a Business 101 book and leaf through it while you're on your summer vacation, even if you are going to have formal training. The more times you see business terms and concepts ahead of your first project, the better job you'll do on the project and higher likelihood of impressing your managers. Especially if you're coming out of undergrad, consider taking a business primer class over the summer if you aren't on a whirlwind tour of Europe. (Dartmouth College, for example, has a "Business Bridge" program for this very purpose.)

- **Keep up with current events.** *The Wall Street Journal* is going to be one of your best resources as a consultant. Also, check out other publications like *The New York Times* business section, *The Financial Times*, and *The Economist*.

You may feel like goofing off the whole summer before you start work, and you probably deserve it. But you also deserve this consulting job and the chance to shine. Shouldn't you make the most of it?

Your first team assignment

The first few weeks at a consulting firm are a crash course in teamwork, and job seekers often underestimate the extent to which collaboration determines a project's success. A common misperception is that consultants sit down with corporate vice presidents, tell them what to do and watch the client's metamorphosis. The truth is that nothing gets accomplished without extensive discussion, countless status meetings and plenty of ad-hoc brainstorming sessions where everyone involved works feverishly to build a consensus.

Over the course of your career in consulting, you will be a member of many teams, often simultaneously. At a client site, for example, you may be working on an implementation team while also sitting down with a proposal team to generate new work. Additionally, you might be working on an "internal" team to develop new community service programs for your own firm. In the course of your workday, you could interact with as many as six different teams, all with different objectives and time commitments. If you have an aversion to meetings, or if you envision a career defined by isolated thinking and long stretches of time without any human interaction, mainstream consulting probably isn't the right choice for you. (If this is really the case, take a look at economics or litigation consulting, where the amount of client interaction is low relative to other sorts of consulting.)

Close quarters, high pressure

Since you'll depend on your client for your office space, be prepared to work in non-lavish conditions. At one client site, your project team may have limited access to conference rooms and be forced to hold team meetings in a cubicle. At another client site, your team may be sharing a single office with no windows and very little space. On other occasions you might find yourselves working out of someone's hotel room regularly. Part of your job will be to learn to be productive with frequent interruptions. More often than not, you will share limited technical resources such as Internet access, VPN connections, printers, copiers, fax machines and wired phones.

It all comes with the nature of the job. Consultants are high-priced migrant workers; they must know how to pack their bags, move to another location and set up shop, all in the blink of an eye and with little choice in the matter. But whether they are working in a crowded office space, a hotel suite late at night or on a flight home, good consultants develop a set of behaviors that makes their jobs much easier.

Some coping tips:

- Take personal calls on your cell phone, away from the project team.
- If you are frustrated with a software program, take a walk and come back with a positive outlook.
- Speak only when necessary in order to keep the noise down in the project room.
- Keep your work space uncluttered.

These simple rules can improve a project's efficiency and the quality of life for your fellow consultants.

Know the objectives

Most productive meetings address a set of objectives, assign individual tasks to support the objectives and set timelines for completion. While this process is fairly routine in a consultant's workweek, the abundance of meetings can have a deadening effect; consultants can spend more time thinking about their mountain of pending work than the actual meeting they are attending.

Walking away from a meeting with only a vague idea of its objectives can lead to a variety of problems, not the least of which is having to meet all over again. Consulting firms operate on tight schedules. Project managers generally do not tolerate having to repeat critical directives, because they are pressed for time and need each component of the team to produce solid results.

Once a meeting is brought to a close, you should walk away with a notepad filled with key points from the discussion and a specific list of your own "to do" items. If you are unclear about a certain portion of the meeting, you should raise the issue immediately, rather than spend your time guessing how to proceed. For each and every meeting, no matter how irrelevant it seems, your attention to detail can make or break your performance on the project team. Don't expect anyone to keep you awake. Fellow consultants are bogged down with their own assignments, and even though they may engage you in small talk, the expectation is that you will deliver results—on time and consistent with the original objectives.

Whatever it takes

If consulting firms seem demanding when trying to meet deadlines, the clients can be downright unforgiving. At the start of every project, the thought of missing deadlines simply does not occur to consultants, nor does the prospect of creating anything but high-quality deliverables. The ugly reality is that executives (both clients and consulting partners) do not always budget enough time or allot enough resources to meet the client's expectations. The result is that consultants must bring a "whatever it takes" attitude to work every day.

If a 60-hour workweek doesn't appear to be enough to get your required work done, then you add on more hours. If a printer breaks down on the night before a big presentation, then you have to find one, even if it means a late-night drive to Kinko's. Sometimes, during the end of projects, you will squeeze massive amounts of work into small timeframes, and you may have to pull an all-nighter or two. These things happen in consulting, and consulting firms expect that you will take it all in stride. You do have some latitude with regard to personal time, but when important deadlines approach, getting out of an assignment is nearly impossible.

The good news is that never-say-die attitudes are contagious, and the longer you work in a consulting firm, the more you begin to appreciate spending time with people who value results so highly. People who leave the consulting profession are often disappointed to learn that their new company employs a more laissez-faire approach to everything it does. The consulting industry's sharp attention to deadlines is both its curse and its strength. Consultants initially bemoan the fact that their job is so demanding, but they often grow to love that very facet of it and, in some cases, see it as justification for never switching careers.

Communicating with your team

Sometimes your team will go into head-down mode, where people are working independently on PowerPoint slides or financial models. As a new consultant, you want to take responsibility for updating your team leaders frequently on where you are with your work. Certainly, they will always want to have a best estimate of their project status. But this will help you, too, because the team leader has experience that you don't, and he or she will likely have some useful suggestions. Once a day is probably fine for an update.

When you are away from your team (say, on a Friday, when all team members are usually in their home office), use voice mail for updates and questions. Most consulting firms communicate as a voice mail culture, meaning that the equivalent to calling a person directly is to leave a voice mail. The recipient can simply hit the "reply" command to respond. Use voice mail for issues of medium urgency, and use e-mail when you can wait 24 hours or more for a response. By the same token, try to reply to each voice mail within two hours or so of its delivery.

Make sure your e-mail doesn't pile up, especially for your project work. To get yourself started on the right foot, play a little game with yourself: Give yourself no more than 24 hours to respond to every work e-mail, and buy yourself a little gift (a latte, for example) for every 10 you successfully respond to on time.

Ask lots of questions

Did one of your junior high teachers waggle his finger at your and claim, "The only stupid question is the one that's never asked?" Remember, you are a new consultant and you are not expected to know anything. If you are fresh out of college, you are not expected to know what a discount rate or DCF is. At MBA or lateral hire levels, you may have never seen a decision tree before. If you feel at all self-conscious about asking silly questions, you'd better stop it right now. Ask away! Internally, consulting is entirely about mentorship and grooming new consultants, and Q&A is the only way to learn.

At the beginning of your first few projects, take a minute during the kickoff meeting to remind your team members that you are still new to the firm, and you would like to set the expectation that you will be asking the team members lots of questions. This is a really good step to take because (1) it shows that you are proactive about learning and doing a great job and (2) your more senior team members will be prepared to help you and not be surprised or frustrated when you come to them for help.

One great way to make sure you ask and answer your questions is to keep a question journal. Devote a couple of pages in your notebook to this task. When something comes up, write it down, whether it's about your firm's methodology, an industry term or how to find the online time tracking system.

Once a day, flip through the questions and figure out which ones make sense to ask. Don't forget to jot the answer down next to the question when you're done.

It also helps to have a "buddy" in the firm who can be your go-to resource for mundane things like voice mail or expense guidelines. Many firms will actually assign you a buddy for this reason. If you are not assigned one, figure out who you feel most comfortable talking with and ask that person directly if he or she wouldn't mind being your resource for all things mundane. Again, the point of this isn't to get permission, but to set the expectation with the person that you will be coming to them for help.

Armed and dangerous

As a high-priced migrant worker, you need to be prepared to migrate from hotel to hotel, client to client and plane to plane. We suggest you make a habit of always keeping a little more than the essentials with you in your briefcase—you'll never know when you might need something.

Here's a partial list of items that consultants usually pack in carry-on luggage:

- Laptop (supplied by your company)
- A Dopp kit of electronics and accessories. A well-outfitted kit may include the following:
    - Power supply for your laptop
    - A set of power plug adapters for foreign travel
    - Cell phone power adapter
    - Blackberry power adapter
    - Retractable Ethernet cable
    - Retractable phone cable (sometimes these come in combination with Ethernet cables)
    - USB flash memory stick for exchanging files
    - Blank CD RWs
    - Wireless PC card (if your laptop isn't wireless ready)
    - Spare laptop battery
    - USB mouse
    - Kryptonite cable lock and key for your laptop
    - Scientific calculator

- Pens and pencils, highlighter, flip chart markers
- Writing paper or notebooks
- Lots of Post-it notepads
- Empty file folders (you will start collecting documents from day one of your engagement)
- Portable desk supplies (stapler, staple remover, tape dispenser)
- Plenty of business cards

Sound crazy? It's probably overkill for your first day on the job. Imagine, though, a late-night crunch period in your hotel room and wishing you had a stapler to bind up your presentation, that you finally found an Ethernet port but were missing a cable, or that your cell phone ran out of juice and you didn't have your power adapter with you. You'll wish you had packed wisely. We know some consultants who have brought things like a portable laser printer, screen projector or an Ethernet connection sharing hub with them on the job.

Getting Staffed

Now that you have a consulting job, guess what? Your job search, in essence, begins all over again. That's because your first few assignments can be critical to your future at your firm. One frequent danger is pigeonholing. (The danger of this tends to be greater at larger consulting firms.) Complete an Excel-based training module about the programming language VBA (Visual Basic for Applications, which can also be used in Microsoft Word, PowerPoint and Access), go on a few successful VBA training assignments and voila!—you're a VBA expert and will be staffed primarily, if not exclusively, on VBA assignments. This sort of thing is fine if you're got a desire to specialize, and even better if you happen to become an "expert" in an area where assignments are diverse and plentiful.

However, there can be drawbacks to such an approach. You might grow to loathe VBA. You might be routinely staffed on assignments where travel is unavoidable. VBA might be the furthest thing from your career goal.

Ask yourself a few questions. Where do you want to work? Do you want to travel? Do you want to work with a particular client? (Many consulting firms have bread-and-butter clients with whom they routinely work.) Do you want to stay with this firm for a few years, or for a career?

If you're not in an area you like—or worse, if you're not getting staffed at all—you have a few options. Do your best to receive training in an area that interests you. Ask those a level above you, as well as your mentor (whether informal or assigned by your firm) if they are aware of any current or upcoming projects in your preferred area. Some consulting companies have internal intranets; don't be shy about using yours to locate projects that interest you and the appropriate contacts.

You may or may not have a representative in human resources who staffs you. Make sure you meet your HR rep and communicate your preferences to him or her regularly. But be warned: While some HR reps are looking out for your best interests, many are simply trying to staff warm bodies without careful thinking. Others may be receiving intense pressure from partners to staff certain people and avoid others specifically on their projects, and therefore you might not get the assignment you want.

If you're new to the organization and know no one, you may not have any options. You may need to take whatever is given to you, be a team player and do the best job you can. If it's not your first choice, in a diplomatic way, make sure your HR rep knows that—to be able to better fit you to your next role. Then use that project to become known as a person who has a great attitude, can do anything and is someone people want to work with.

Even if you despise your project, build relationships with project managers on every project you are staffed on. They are the front lines to the staffing opportunities; they decide who they want to be on their team. Those managers will also support you for promotion and help you navigate the company. Soon, you will be staffed directly on projects by your contacts.

On the Beach

By the time you've worked in consulting for a few months, you'll be very familiar with the expression "on the beach." This simply means that you are not staffed on a client-billable project. The more consultants a firm has on the beach, the lower the firm's utilization rate. In times when clients spend more on consultants, utilization rates can be in the 90 percent range; in economic downturns, the industry's average firm utilization rate can be as low as 50 percent.

Being on the beach is a mixed blessing for consultants. On the plus side, it means you are not traveling, for once, and you can come into the office at 9 a.m. and leave at 5 p.m. On the negative side, it means that you are not gaining any project experience, and the less project experience you have, the less development as a consultant you get, the less likelihood you have of being staffed and the higher chance you face of being let go by your firm when times get tough. So while being on the beach for a little while is a good thing, too much beach time is something you want to avoid.

That said, there are some productive ways you can spend your beach time.

Play catch up

First, allow yourself some time to regroup. Catch up on your expenses and time tracking. Clean your desk. Take care of that health insurance paperwork with your HR folks. Answer those nagging e-mails from a month ago. Everyone needs downtime for such things, and everyone you work with will understand that you deserve it.

Don't feel bad about squeezing in a little personal time over a couple of days for errands. This is a good chance to get back to the dentist or have that physical you've been meaning to get out of the way. Also, you might as well schedule the cable guy to swing by to fix your cable box, so let someone know you're working from home on Tuesday. And you can finally have lunch with your college roommate. Don't go overboard with the personal stuff—just realize that this is a good time to fit a few things in.

Network for new projects

Revisit the mental process you went through the last time you were staffed. What did you get out of your last project? What are your current project goals? What industries would you be interested to work in next? What skills would you like to develop? Be sure to jot these down and keep them on the tip of your tongue, for you will need to start communicating these topics to others.

If you have someone assigned to staff you, let that person know you're available. You will need to start networking for a new project right away. Target a few partners and senior managers and leave them voice mails, letting them know that you are checking in and looking for a new project. If you're in the office, pop by a few desks and see if the partners you know are close to selling a new piece of work, and let them know you're available. Remember that your contacts (partners and senior managers) are busy, so you will need to keep following up with them to see if new opportunities have materialized.

Marketing work

When firms aren't executing consulting engagements, they are working on acquiring them. You can guarantee that the partners selling work will always want help doing so. Such help will usually be in the form of research. You might write up an industry overview and do a competitive assessment. You might create a deck of slides on a potential client and come up with possible issues they are facing that might require the help of a consultancy. Or you might be put to work on a draft of the actual proposal.

Be sure to ask your contacts above if they need help on sales and marketing, and offer your assistance. While they may not always have a live project available for you, they very likely could use your help elsewhere. If you help a partner sell work, he or she will already know that you are familiar with the client and would be likely to staff you on the project.

Internal studies

Many consulting firms put out white papers and articles. Many efforts are the pet projects of just a few people, so opportunities to work on them are few and far between, but sometimes the writers need extra help with research and editing. Find out who manages these efforts from your mentors in the firm. Call up those contacts and ask how you can help. You will probably have some chasing around to do, so keep at it. With luck, you might find yourself working on your company's next *Harvard Business Review* article.

Some larger consulting firms also have intranets where consultants are encouraged to post findings and articles. Go ahead and add your work to the repository—partners looking for consultants with specific expertise may staff you on their projects.

Self-training

If you have looked for new projects, done all the available marketing work, and tried to find internal studies to work on, then you still need to keep yourself busy. This is a great time for self-training. Look over your development goals for the year and take steps to pursue them. For example, is your goal to learn Visual Basic for Applications in Excel and Access? Buy yourself a book and spend six hours a day reading and doing the exercises rigorously. In two weeks or less, you will be reasonably proficient at VBA.

(Keep the extra two hours to continue to network for other internal and external opportunities.) Do you want to gain expertise in the energy field? Spend the time reading trade journals, taking notes and scheduling time with your firm's energy experts to pick their brains.

How many consulting job boards have you visited lately?

(Thought so.)

Use the Internet's most targeted job search tools for consulting professionals.

Vault Consulting Job Board
The most comprehensive and convenient job board for consulting professionals. Target your search by area of consulting, function, and experience level, and find the job openings that you want. No surfing required.

VaultMatch Resume Database
Vault takes match-making to the next level: post your resume and customize your search by area of consulting, experience and more. We'll match job listings with your interests and criteria and e-mail them directly to your inbox.

VAULT
> the most trusted name in career information™

The Consulting Career Path

CHAPTER 9

Training for Consultants

A career in consulting is attractive for many reasons, but few of these are as important to jobseekers as the amount of training they will receive. Unlike industries such as consumer products or pharmaceuticals, where companies funnel investment dollars into product design and research and development, the consulting industry's largest expenditure (apart from staff salaries and overhead) is training. Every year, consulting firms allocate as much as 20 percent of their revenue to internal training programs, and consultants reap the benefits. It is not uncommon for a consultant to spend four to eight weeks per year attending firm-sponsored classes, taking computer-based training programs (CBTs), and studying industry-related literature to improve their performance on the job.

The training requirements in consulting are, by any measure, extensive, and employees who hail from top-ranked schools and prestigious firms find the ongoing skill development not only to be personally satisfying, but also valuable. Headhunters and recruiters for Fortune 500 companies realize how much training consultants receive, and they are willing to pay top dollar for people who have spent considerable time developing their skills.

Orientation training

Over the course of their careers, consultants will encounter two general categories of training: orientation and ongoing training. Orientation training begins soon after new hires walk in the door and greet their assigned human resource representatives. In large firms, most of the orientation training actually occurs in a centralized, distant location; after new hires fill out reams of paperwork at their home office, they board a plane and fly to the firm's massive training campus. Once they check into their assigned rooms, attend a welcome meeting and spend some time getting to know their "classmates" from around the world, they begin a program that will last anywhere from one to four weeks, depending on the firm.

Orientation training is notoriously rigorous and exhausting. New hires spend most of their days working in teams, meeting with firm executives who pose as clients, attending lectures, learning Excel, mocking up PowerPoint slides and completing CBTs. Consulting firms spend millions of dollars each year to prepare new hires for their first few projects and they make sure that, by the end of the training, employees understand just how strenuous consulting can be. Consulting firms do budget in time for rest and relaxation, but such time pales in comparison to the hard work and countless hours of team-based learning. Regardless, most new consultants, despite feeling worn out at the end of each day, find the experience very gratifying. Orientation training may be a rude awakening, but it offers many perks. Where else can recent college graduates work with people from around the world, build lasting friendships and be paid large sums of money to attend class?

Ongoing training

Once consultants get acclimated to living in hotels and working with clients, training requirements reemerge as part of their ongoing development. Every year, experienced consultants complete a curriculum of analytical training, industry-specific seminars, management workshops and a host of other training programs designed to complement on-the-job learning.

Aside from making consultants better at what they do, ongoing training also functions as a tool to gauge how ready employees are for promotion. Indeed, many firms will not promote an employee unless he first completes the required curriculum for that particular year. Consultants, therefore, have a two-part incentive for completing their ongoing training requirements. Not only do they hope to become better consultants, but they want very much to rise through the ranks, make more money and have greater responsibility.

Consulting Job Descriptions and Career Progression

Trying to define and describe the role of a consultant is far from easy. In other professions—lawyer, doctor, accountant—the title says it all. Consultants, however, find themselves attempting to explain their job to people throughout their careers. The individual experience of a consultant varies by firm style, specialization, geographic differences and the many roles within a project. Initially, the analyst (college graduates) and associate (post-MBA) roles involve different skill sets. However, the differences between a second-year analyst and a new associate are less pronounced.

Consulting titles vary by firm (see figure below for just how much they vary at selected firms). Common entry-level titles for recent college grads include associate, consultant and analyst. Typical titles for experienced hires or post-MBAs include associate, senior associate and senior consultant. Distinctions between management titles exist as well—for example, manager, senior manager, director, senior director, managing director, partner, principal, senior partner, managing partner, partner-in-charge, vice president, and senior vice president.

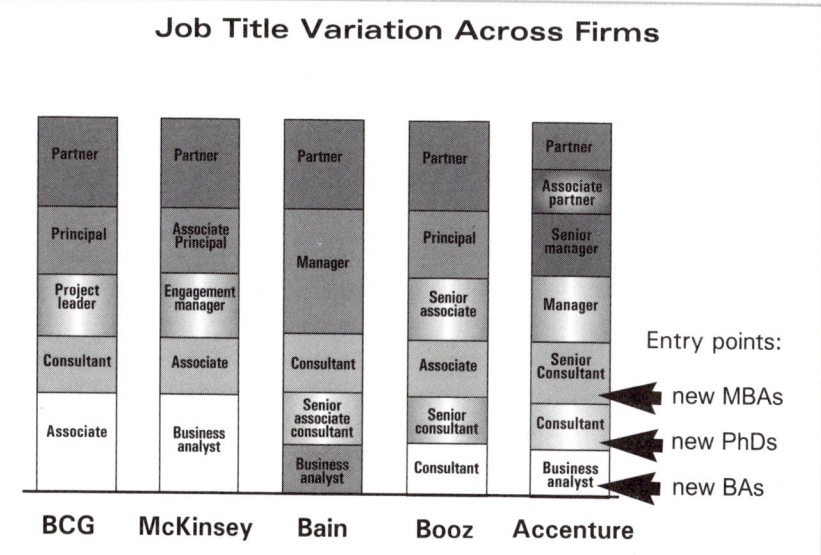

Titles in the consulting world don't mean all that much unless you are familiar with the structure of the particular firm in question. For example, BCG associates don't have an MBA, but a McKinsey associate can be up to three years out of business school. Similarly, an Accenture manager might be 32 years old or so, while a Bain manager might very well be in his late 30s and far more senior in the organization.

Adding to the confusion is the fact that individual firms change their position nomenclature fairly frequently. For instance, BCG partners were known as vice presidents just a couple of years ago. Although the titles in the graph above were accurate at press time, you will want to confirm the title progression for any given firm before you make too many assumptions.

While job titles at consulting firms differ, the levels and promotion path across firms are remarkably similar: entry-level/undergraduate (analyst), mid-level/MBA (associate), management-level (manager) and the director/partner-level. The primary purpose of each role in your career is to prepare for the next.

The analyst role (pre-MBA)

Analysts gather and analyze data, draw conclusions from their analyses and insert their results into the "stories" the team presents to the client.

Analysts spend their first two or three years learning the consulting ropes. They join projects that span multiple industries, functions and technologies. They start to build reputations for being reliable, spectacular, insightful or quick. They also start to understand what areas of specialization they prefer.

Analysts typically spend two to three years at consulting firms before getting an MBA or abandoning the field altogether. Some consulting firms now promote leading analysts directly to the associate level. At some of the top consulting firms (Bain, BCG and McKinsey, for instance) the typical analyst path includes business school before promotion to associate. In rare cases, a sterling analyst is given the option of promotion without business school. In other firms (e.g., Booz Allen Hamilton), analysts routinely win promotions to associate after two to three years. Among the Big Four's IT consulting practices, an MBA is not necessarily a prerequisite for promotion. In fact, the pursuit of an MBA may be encouraged or discouraged, depending on the consultant's area of specialization.

Analysts are selected for inquiring minds, quantitative aptitude and willingness to learn, rather than any specific industry or functional experience. Most consulting firms offer training programs, but the main learning occurs on the job. Analysts come to play more important roles within the firm as they gain experience.

When client members are involved in the team, an advanced analyst might also manage the client's work on the team to some extent. Take advantage of such circumstances as your opportunity to shine.

The associate role (post-MBA)

The associate role evolves rapidly as the consultant gets up to speed and earns the confidence of a more senior consultant. At the beginning, the associate's role might differ from the analyst's if the associate is on an accelerated career track; otherwise, the first year can look identical. A year or so later, however, the associate manages the team's work (client members and analysts) and day-to-day client relationships. She or he generates hypotheses, analyzes phases and structures (and occasionally delivers) presentations at client review meetings.

More often than not, associate consultants in a large, diversified consulting firm focus on their desired specialization (usually industry) after two to three years. Ten years ago, specialization was encouraged earlier on in one's career; now new MBA consultants are encouraged for the most part to stick to being a "generalist" for a little while before choosing a specific focus. During this period, associates also begin to learn management skills, as they are responsible for managing the team's results and activities hands-on. Networking—both within and outside the firm—becomes increasingly important, because associates will often have to work with other consulting teams (e.g., a reengineering team working with an IT team, or working with another consulting firm for the same client).

Sometimes there's a senior associate role after a consultant has been an associate for a couple of years. This role recognizes the associate as having progressed beyond the entry level, but not to the level where they can be left alone to run the day-to-day operations of an engagement.

After two to four years as an associate, the consultant is promoted to a manager position. Consultants at this level manage and develop the day-to-day relationships with key client personnel. They also manage the team's activities in an official capacity. The key differences in this role are the need to step back from the details more often and to manage staff. Unlike the associate who manages the tangibles, managers oversee the team, resolve major issues and make key decisions.

Following manager comes the senior manager position (again, all titles vary by firm), where the consultant begins developing more off-engagement relationships with clients and prospecting for new business. At this stage, the senior manager is also given a broader range of projects to oversee at a higher level. Networking at this level is especially important, since many firms eventually ask their other lines of business to evaluate your partnership worthiness. Also, a large part of partnership status depends on the amount of business you are able to build.

The partner role

The ultimate aspiration of a career consultant is to achieve the partner (or principal) position. Most consulting firms are LLPs or LLCs, with the partners being partners in the legal sense of the word, each owning a significant equity stake in the firm. Compensation for partners is overwhelmingly tied to both their individual performance in drumming up business as well as the firm's fortunes. Being a partner requires building and maintaining client relationships and developing the intellectual capital of the firm. Most consultancies operate as partnerships. A promotion to partner normally involves a hefty increase in compensation, as partners contribute directly to the firm's profits. Many firms have upped the ante by lowering their partners' base salaries and tying compensation more directly to how much the partner sells. This creates a strong incentive for the partner to sell new work, though it also creates lots of pressure and sometimes competition among partners.

Some partnerships also have the equivalent of a director position. The director normally declines taking the risks and rewards associated with partnership, but shares the same responsibilities. (This position is known as associate partner.)

Few consultants who enter the field ever make it to partner, as most of them are either let go from their firms or leave to pursue other opportunities (often to reduce the burden of consulting on their family life). The following exhibit illustrates typical odds of becoming a consulting partner:

The Long Road to Partnership

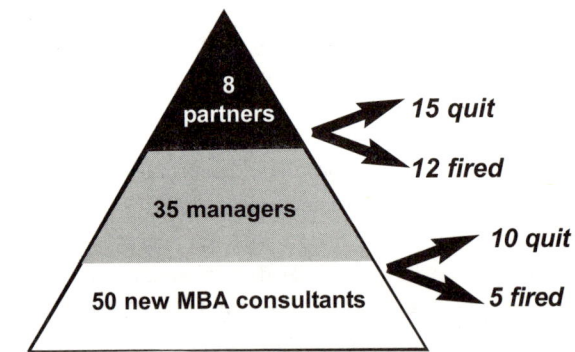

Note: In this example, of those consultants who didn't leave voluntarily, there was a 32% chance to make it to partner.

The potential to make partner varies enormously from firm to firm. As a general guideline, you've got something like a 5:1 shot of both avoiding termination and being willing to stick it out. The odds are better than that in a growing firm, because there will be more partner slots available by the time you're up for promotion to that level. Remember that it's the income jump at partner level that people refer to when they talk about the financial rewards of a consulting career.

Internships in consulting

Many of you are reading this guide as a sophomore or junior in college, a first-year MBA or a graduate student with more than a year left in your degree program. In these cases, you will be looking for an internship. Simply put, an internship is a temporary position, where consulting firms hire students and other employees for a specified period of time. In addition, because so many of the interns are typically students, and the bulk of students do not take classes during the summer, most consulting internships occur during the summer months.

For the most part, a consulting internship isn't all that different from the entry-level consulting you would get after you earn your degree. Still, there are a few distinctions worth noting to applicants.

Why internships exist

Most of the large consulting firms have an annual summer internship program. One reason is that summer internships are a highly effective form of recruiting for everyone involved. A summer internship is a chance for the firm to evaluate you for a couple of months on the job before choosing to extend you a full-time offer. It is also a golden, extended opportunity for the firm to sell you on its interesting projects, work-life balance, and culture. Finally, interns are an incredibly effective form of word-of-mouth advertising. If you have a good experience at the firm, you will no doubt tell all of your classmates about how great the firm is and why they should work there.

In addition, consulting interns are a source of cost-efficient labor for the firm. For instance, interns often are paid less than their full-time equivalents. Even though an undergrad intern might do the work of a first-year analyst for a summer, she or he would probably get paid a little less per month than would the first-year analyst. In addition, hiring a consultant for a summer is cheaper for the firm than bringing on a permanent hire. (Note that because the intern doesn't contribute as much value to the client as a full-timer, the consulting firm usually bills out the intern to the client at zero cost—this makes the consulting firm bear the full cost of the intern.)

That said, the internship is a fantastic opportunity for the employee for a number of reasons. The biggest advantage is that an internship gives the student a great inside track to a full-time offer. In most internship programs, the highest performing interns are given an offer to join the firm on a full-time basis after graduation.

A typical summer internship

Most consulting summer internships last eight to 12 weeks. A number of summer internship programs start with a week of training to start; typical topics include firm history and values, problem solving, technology training (PowerPoint and Excel for management consultants, and systems and programming tools for technology consultants) and presentation skills. If you are interning with a large consulting firm, you will probably have some sort of formalized interactive classroom training along these lines. The smaller firms will often train you on the job instead.

During the first week, an HR professional at the firm will attempt to staff each of the interns, attempting to match the available supply of projects with the interns' interests. Not all interns are staffed immediately, but because they are a priority in the staffing queue, most are staffed within the first two weeks.

The projects are, for the most part, real engagements. Because you are an intern, your start date probably won't coincide with the project kickoff, so you really could join the project at any time.

Typical tasks for the undergraduate intern are not that different from those of the first-year analyst, and the job of the MBA summer intern is similar to that of the first-year associate. The main difference is that because the intern is a temporary hire, his or her work needs to be completed within a defined period of time that may not coincide with the actual project completion. So, by and large, interns will be assigned clearly segmentable project work, like the secondary research of 15 competitors, a small market-sizing spreadsheet model or a specific set of PowerPoint slides. MBA interns might take on additional responsibility, such as more extensive financial modeling. (Please refer to the "On the Job" section of this guide for a description of typical tasks.)

Many internship programs involve at least one performance review, at the end of the summer. Some programs have a midsummer review as well. This can be helpful because it gives the intern a chance to improve his or her work before offers are made. If you don't have a formal review planned as part of your internship, be proactive in asking for one.

Finally, since as an intern you are still technically a recruit, you will likely be wined and dined. Perks include free fine dining, baseball games, attaches and concerts. In recent years, firms have scaled back these perks considerably for cost reasons, but interns will probably get a nice meal or two during the summer, regardless.

Landing a summer internship in consulting

The recruiting process for summer internships is identical to that for full-time offers. The only difference is timing. The summer internship recruiting cycle typically starts in January, whereas often consulting firms hire for full-time in the fall for the following fall. Be sure to check with your school's career office for timing and procedures.

Be warned that today, due to the economic slowdown, there are fewer available internships for undergraduates and MBAs than in recent years. A compounding affect is the seasonality of the consulting industry. The summer months typically result in the lowest spending on consultants of any part of the year. Combine this with the overall economic slowdown, and we have a reduced incentive for firms to take on a full load of summer internships. At the same time, firms are significantly scaling back their on-campus recruiting efforts. Keep in mind that internships are more competitive than permanent jobs. Some firms are hiring the vast majority of full-time hires from their internship classes.

Treat the consulting internship job search like an off-campus job search. Do the research on firms and contact your targets to see if they are hiring interns. Also, if you have flexibility in your campus schedule, see if you can work during the spring or fall instead, when there will be fewer students competing for scarce internship spots. If the firm is local, see if you can work part-time during a semester.

Tips on being an effective summer intern

Full-time offers for summer interns are almost a given in a good economic climate. In contrast, during a downturn, it's probable that nobody in the intern class will receive an offer. Regardless of whether you are gunning for a full-time offer, we recommend you focus on making the most out of your summer internship:

- Ask to be put on an engagement with travel. You really want to make sure you will like consulting, so push yourself. If you try to get on a project with no travel, you will not have a realistic picture of consulting (since that would be the exception, not the norm).

- Collect business cards. You will be meeting lots of consultants, and it will difficult to remember them all. Try to grab their business card at some point and make a few notes on the back. In the future, you can touch base with them and have a few tidbits to remind them who you are.

- Attend as many social events as possible. Treat the summer as one long networking event. You want to meet as many consultants of all levels at firm, and you will want to stay in touch with the other interns you meet.

- Set up Friday one-on-one meetings. Again, you are building your network. Try to meet up with a wide range of consultants, including partners. Friday is a great day for this, because consultants tend to be in their home office on Fridays. Grab coffee with some of the newer consultants to get the inside scoop on the firm.

Performance assessment

Performance assessment is a critical tool for your career development and the firm's success. Usually, someone one level above you on "larger" projects reviews your performance at the end of the project or phase. (By most definitions, a "larger" project involves a minimum of 80 hours, though the exact figure differs by firm.) Some firms require self-assessments as well. The reviews are designed to evaluate your progress and any development needs you might have.

Most firms conduct official reviews of all consultants on an annual or semi-annual basis. Management goes off-site and/or holds meetings that can last several days. While each firm's practices vary, most generally use this time to measure your performance against your peers. Based on where you fall in the lineup, management determines your salary increase and evaluates your readiness for promotion.

To ensure that you fall near the top of the list, document and self-promote every success or instance in which you excelled beyond expectations. Solicit your clients for letters of gratitude or recommendation for your personnel file. Train yourself in areas of interest to you and let it be known that you are an "expert." Conduct research and analysis studies on little-known fields within your industry or service line, and (just out of the goodness of your heart) share the information with your colleagues. Just as you did extra credit work in school, make public the initiatives you introduced to differentiate yourself from your peers. In short, going the extra mile in all aspects of your career gets you noticed.

Your image can help or hurt you. The most competent consultant can be overlooked if his or her peers are not as shy about showcasing their best work. An enthusiastic attitude can only work for you, yet you might feel uncomfortable about boasting, or feel adamantly that your work should speak for itself. If so, find some other way to let your competence and high standards of excellence be known to your superiors.

Your performance is measured by criteria similar to those first used to hire you—analytical and quantitative skills, teamwork and leadership. As you progress, the evaluation emphasis shifts toward your people management skills and client relationship capabilities, including your ability to sell. While matching your perceptions of your performance with your managers', address your development needs, organize your training and set your goals.

Office politics

Office politics is a fact of life in any corporate environment, though the consulting industry is no worse, and in many ways better, than other industries in this regard. Frequent reviews and performance assessments, a reliance on teamwork and the relative lack of hierarchical frills all help downplay office politics in the consulting environment. Perhaps the most politically charged aspect of the consulting life is the competition to be staffed on engagements.

Consulting firms all have an official process by which consultants are staffed on projects. This may be done through a central staffing office or by a senior consultant at the firm. However, all consulting firms have a parallel black market, an unofficial system where consultants are either chosen directly for projects by their directors, or where consultants network and approach the leaders of their desired engagements directly.

Understand the unofficial process from the start and play the game with the best of them—after all, your projects and the directors for whom you work can make or break your consulting experience. Getting on choice assignments means less probability of being pigeonholed unwillingly, and a greater probability of visibility.

Project staffing addresses conflicting needs from various constituencies. On the one hand, the firm wants associates and analysts to gain broad exposure to different industries and project types. On the other hand, both clients and partners prefer to staff projects with consultants who have some experience in the area, and directors often request specific consultants whom they have found reliable on prior engagements. Moreover, clients' needs sometimes take precedence, depending on market demands. This complicated situation results in elaborate compromises between your firm's management and the client, which means that your personal needs are sometimes overlooked.

To stack the assignment cards in your favor, tap unofficial sources of information about upcoming projects. The best source of information is management (from either your current or previous studies) or your mentor. Learn about projects that you would potentially want to work on, and express an interest up front to these senior people. Tell as many people as you can about your areas of interest. When a relevant study comes up, ask them to remember you as an enthusiastic team member. While remembering you does not guarantee you a position, it certainly helps.

You can also volunteer to help with knowledge development or intellectual capital work being done within your firm. Practice development leaders constantly search for additional help and jump at the chance to get willing consultants involved. In addition to developing your understanding of the industry, volunteering exposes you to senior consultants. Additionally, you gain valuable skills and knowledge. As your value to the firm increases, your value to clients also increases, which means your negotiating power increases proportionally.

Mentors: Top-level Backing

Soon after orientation at your firm, expect to be assigned to a formal mentor. Your mentor is responsible for your success within the firm. Recognize the usefulness of this relationship from the start. Your mentor is responsible for your development, so speak candidly with him or her about your career aspirations, assignment preferences and development needs. Your mentor also acts as an informal communication channel with you and other management. He or she relays impressions of your performance and how others in the firm perceive you. Think of your mentor alternately as your champion, spy, ally and bouncer within your firm.

In addition to mentors, many firms offer "buddies"—professionals who are slightly more experienced than you (often a year or so more advanced) and available to assist with day-to-day details, like how to fill out an expense sheet. Often, these buddies are good first-line mentors. While they might offer less insight because of their limited work experience, they make excellent sounding boards, generally have more time than managers and usually want to help you.

If both your assigned mentor and buddy lack time, information or attention for you, consider seeking other mentors. Still, maintain an "official" assigned mentor/buddy relationship, unless your chemistry leads to unbearable resentment or negativity. (It only helps you to have more people in your corner.) Develop an informal mentor network with those who specialize in an area of interest to you or share some other commonality. Seek out those with whom you find communication, rapport and understanding to be natural.

Just remember that your mentor/buddy is not necessarily your friend. Indeed, some prefer to keep mentoring relationships separate from personal and/or professional friendships, and you might feel it is better to keep the relationship's capacity strictly official. We've heard of stories where the mentor has indeed become a trusted advisor to the new consultant, and we've also heard of stories where the mentor took information that was to be held strictly in confidence, shared it with other senior members of the firm, and got the new consultant fired the next day. Be careful.

Exit Strategies

Bain often calls its consulting positions a "springboard" to an exciting career. Indeed, if you are not excited about the idea of selling work 100 percent of the time as a consulting partner, you will eventually be leaving consulting.

What you might do later

As we mentioned before, many analysts in consulting move on to business school or abandon the field altogether. Some of them return to their employer (the lucky ones get tuition paid for), while others move to other consulting firms or even change careers. If you're an analyst interested in graduate school, take the time to consider the possibility of a different graduate program. It is easy to get caught up in thinking that business school is the next obvious thing, because it most definitely is. Simply make sure that you wouldn't be more interested in law school, a teaching certification or a PhD in your favorite college subject.

A lot of associates who leave their firms take positions in corporate strategy, marketing or business development. Some find employment with former clients. Not all associates who leave their firms abandon consulting, however; many of them move to other consulting firms in an attempt to "trade up," in the form of a different brand name or a faster promotion to a better title.

Leaving gracefully

Whatever you choose to do to follow your days at your current consulting firm, be it another consulting firm or graduate school, you never, ever want to burn your bridges, no matter how bitter you may be or how anxious you are to leave. What if your new job turns out to be a disaster and you want to return to your old firm? What if the market for new PhDs in English fizzles when you graduate? Suppose you graduate from the MBA program in a recession? What if you need a reference—or even a job—from your old employer?

When you have secured your new position or admission to school, speak individually to your official and unofficial mentors in the firm—all of them that mean something to you. If they don't know already, tell them about your new opportunity and why you have chosen it. Then, explain how grateful you are for the opportunities you have had at your current firm, and especially for that person's generosity and guidance. The week you leave, try to schedule a couple of key one-on-one lunches. Even if you are excited to leave the firm, you want to make sure people remember you. When you get to your new destination, send your updated contact information to your key sponsors at your old firm. Try to keep in touch by phone or e-mail once every six months or so to start.

You may never go back to your former employer again, and that's fine. But having taken the small steps to exit with grace, you will always be able to call on your former employer as a reference.

Our Survey Says: The Consulting Lifestyle

CHAPTER 10

For people considering a career in consulting, few factors matter as much as the lifestyle. The demands of heavy travel, long workdays and months of living out of suitcases are enough to drive many job seekers away. For others, however, the thrill of the constantly changing business environments, the frequent flyer miles and the chance to work with new project teams are too much to pass up. Consulting may be a grind, but it remains a prestigious way to make a living, a great training ground for senior management positions in Fortune 500 companies and a ticket to see the world.

Salary and benefits

Relative to many other business career paths, consulting salaries are fairly attractive. But they aren't as attractive as you might think. They are generally higher than for standard internal corporate jobs, but well below the salaries of investment bankers, corporate lawyers and many doctors, since most consultants do not go onto become a partner. (See the following exhibit for a rudimentary salary comparison.)

Comparative Income Trajectories

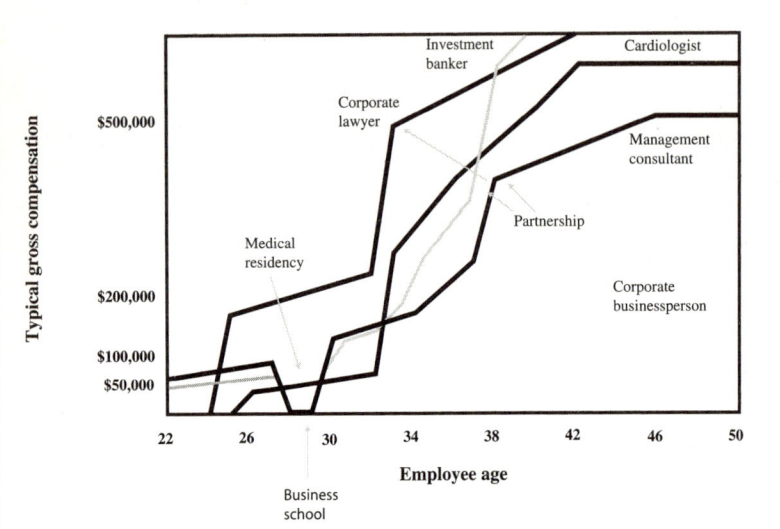

Management consultants have the potential to make much higher incomes than businesspeople who go the corporate route. However, a substantial divergence in salary doesn't really occur until the consultant makes partner, which may or may not happen.

Just after business school, doctors are still in training and make slightly less than the typical management consultant, but most specialties soon leave the consulting income level far behind. Corporate lawyers start practicing at a much earlier age than do consultants, due to not needing work experience to get into graduate school—not only are their salaries substantially higher, but they get those high salaries at a younger age. Investment banking salaries start escalating well above the consultant pay scale soon after business school, and climb dramatically higher than most any other business job once the partner level (known in banking as "managing director") is reached.

The point is that management consulting is indeed handsomely remunerated relative to many other business roles, but within the broader context of possible professions, it is not the best way to get rich.

But on an absolute basis, salaries are pretty darn good. Starting salaries for undergraduates range between $45,000 to $60,000, depending on the firm, plus a target individual or firm-based performance bonus of 10 to 20 percent. In years when firms are hiring in larger numbers, they may also offer a one-time signing bonus of a few thousand dollars to compete for the top candidates.

Salaries for MBA hires are always in flux. Until the 2001-2003 economic downturn, big-name firms like McKinsey, BCG and Accenture had been pushing base salary offers to newly minted MBAs into the $120,000 range, with sign-on bonuses as high as $20,000 to $30,000 and target bonuses near $30,000 (i.e., first-year total comp of $170-180K). In some cases, MBA candidates have gotten their entire business school tuition paid for—on top of all the money thrown at them on day one. Then, during the 2001-2003 downturn, base salaries sank down to about $100,000 plus a $15,000 performance bonus and no signing bonus (i.e., first-year total comp of $115K). That down cycle turned out to be a semi-permanent salary correction. In 2008, the median base salary for a "top-tier" firm has bounced part-way back to right around $110,000 with a signing bonus of $20,000 and target performance bonus of $20,000 (i.e., total first-year comp of $150K). Expect these numbers to continue fluctuating and to be different by the time you actually interview for a firm yourself.

Consulting salaries become really attractive when you look beyond the first year and consider annual raises. At top consulting firms, standard raises often start in the 8 to 10 percent range and escalate into the 15 to 20 percent range for high performers. Consultants also stand to benefit from profit-sharing programs, year-end bonuses or overtime pay, depending on the firm.

The benefit packages vary from firm to firm, but are generally pretty compelling. At the large firms, it's completely reasonable to expect fully-paid, top-notch medical, dental, life and disability insurance plans. A good benefits package also includes a generous and easy-to-exercise parental leave policy, and fully-matched 401(k) plan. Icing on the cake could include discounts on a host of other goodies: gym memberships, new car purchases, museum entry, movie tickets and even processing home mortgages. At smaller firms, you are more likely to receive partially-subsidized insurance, and fewer bells and whistles in your benefits package. Standard fare for time off when you first start is three weeks paid vacation, nine to 11 paid holidays, and two to three floating holidays to accommodate multiple religions.

Per diems make a difference

Per diems are cost-of-living payments that consultants in some firms receive while staffed on an out-of-town assignment. Consulting firms realize that when a consultant is away on assignment, cost-of-living factors are higher than would be normal. Out-of-town projects require that you spend long hours at the client site, forcing you to eat out all the time, and making it hard to perform simple tasks like doing your laundry. Some consulting firms pick up the slack for you on these tasks in the form of a per diem, while others just have you submit individual receipts for (possible) reimbursement.

Per diems are given to you as part of your paycheck, and they can range from $20 to $50 per day, depending on the firm and your project's location. Over the course of a two-week period, an allotment of per diems can add up to a few hundred dollars; to the extent that it actually costs you less than this to eat and maintain your life away from home, part of that feels like extra money to your bottom line. Over the course of a year, your effective salary can grow by more than $10,000—a nice way for firms to placate consultants who are working far from home.

Not all firms use the per diem approach, so be sure to check with your firm's HR accountants to understand not only what the policies are.

A reality check

All this said, don't find yourself sucked into consulting strictly for money, because it isn't quite as good as it sounds. Why? The fact is that it's rather expensive to maintain the lifestyle necessary to succeed in a consulting career. There are lots of hidden costs of being a consultant over and above the reimbursable project expenses. Your cell phone bill will be enormous, and may or may not be subsidized by your employer. You likely pay for your own high-speed Internet at home, which is a requirement for you to be able to function in your role. The same goes for the periodicals you need to read, the clothes you need to wear and coif you must maintain to a high standard, the late-night dry cleaning pick-ups because you're working late, and the cost of eating out because you are home too late to grocery shop or cook. There will be no using the public library for you—if you want to read a book, you need to buy it. Most consultants we know have a steady stream of UPS packages arriving at their front doors—they simply never go shopping for anything, be it clothes, gifts or household items. If you need to go somewhere, you probably skip public transit and take a cab.

In addition, your career trajectory is highly dependent on knowing the right people, having them like you and continuing to network all the time—this involves dinners out, drinks at happy hour and generally being a social person who is out and about at events. For example, in most environments, your colleagues will likely be going out to grab a sandwich at lunchtime (and likely eating it at their computers)—you might feel that you can't afford a $10 sandwich and drink day in and out ($2,500 per year, or about $4,000 of your gross income), but bringing your own bag lunch and eschewing the group walk to the deli makes you strange, creating one chip in the image of team-oriented consultant you are trying to create.

Marriott, sweet Marriott

Needless to say, experienced consultants are experts at hotel living. But most consultants end up in hotel rooms where the quality of life can grow stale very quickly.

Because you tend to fly into a city in the morning and go straight to the client site, you'll probably first set foot in your hotel at the end of the day. (So be sure to have your assistant book your hotel room with late check-in guaranteed.) Generally, because you're mostly on client site, your hotel room becomes a place where you spend very little time; it'll basically be a refuge for sleeping, showering and changing your clothes. Nonetheless, everything in the hotel, every detail, begins to take on a much greater importance than you ever expected. Size of the room. Sitting area. TV stations. Fax capabilities and location of electrical outlets (for your laptop). In-house restaurants. Workout facilities. Food quality. And (lest we forget) loyalty point programs.

But the choice of hotel is either completely arbitrary or utter crucial relative to your project experience, depending on your value system. Project managers usually provide guidance on where the team will stay in the form of either a price cap or a preferred hotel based on client or consulting firm discounts. If you have a choice, though, here are some nominal considerations in choosing a hotel:

- Is it important that you stay close to the client site? Reasons for this might be: lots of early morning meetings; lots of late nights; good conglomeration of restaurants and bars near the client site; a solid discount for guests affiliated with the client. Staying close to the client site is not always the most important thing. If you don't always need to be close to the client site and you're going to be on a client engagement for an extended period of time, you might as well pick the hotel within 20 minutes that has the right combination of services and amenities for you.

- Do you have a price guideline per night? Ask your project leader for guidance on this. Without better information, there are unwritten ceilings on prices per night out there: less than $100 for a small city or rural area, less than $200 for a midsized city and less than $300 for a large city. You want to be very careful about not overdoing it on the hotel stars—imagine having to justify staying at the Four Seasons to your frugal Houston client!

- Are you a member of any loyalty point programs for hotels? Obviously this will factor into your decisions. You'll be happy if the client has a couple of choices for you in terms of preferred hotels with discounts, because you'll probably wind up with one of them belonging to your favorite loyalty program. But this needs to be a secondary consideration after the first two above.

When they have time at night, consultants tend to be very picky about what they eat. The gregarious types try to avoid room service whenever possible. Getting out of the hotel, venturing to new restaurants and trying new things at night are great ways to enhance the life of a consulting engagement. If you only see the client site and the inside of your hotel room, it can wear on you. Generally speaking, try to get outside, take a drive and see the locale in which you are living. Change of scenery can make a big difference. On the other hand, if you're the type that needs to recharge his or her batteries solo, don't feel bad about relying on room service—just keep in mind that it can be pretty expensive and it's good to mix up your dining options with some delivery choices that the front desk can give you.

Planes, trains and automobiles

Not all consulting firms have scaled back the time their employees spend away from the home office, but the competition to offer new hires an attractive work/life balance is much fiercer than it was 10 years ago; at a minimum, most firms now practically guarantee that consultants will spend Friday at the home office. Even so, consulting is still about travel, whether to a client site, home again after a long week in a distant city, or to training facilities around the world.

Of course, frequent flyer and hotel loyalty points can ease the burden. Spend a few years in consulting, and the miles you earn will cover nearly every personal trip that you take during your employment as a consultant. You'll probably have the status to fly with first class upgrades for a couple of years, too. For some, though, having that status on all those airlines is a sign of failure, because it means you're traveling way too much.

What class of airline seat should you book? Ask the partner on your project for guidance if your firm doesn't have a policy. A common one is flying economy domestically and business class (not first) for international flights; default to this system in the absence of better information.

Another concern is how you will commute to the client site once you arrive. Will you need a rental car? Will you travel to the site by train? Do you have to carpool with other project team members? These issues impact your quality of life once you reach the client site. You may have to share a rental car to keep costs down (and accordingly have to stay at the same hotel as other project team members). Again, ask the partner on your project for guidance on this.

Take a long vacation

Consulting offers similar vacation packages as other business jobs—but it may be difficult to actually take that vacation time. You can typically expect three weeks of paid vacation per year when you start. Vacation is usually doled out based on tenure with the company, rather than seniority, so new MBAs and new BAs are typically in the same boat. After a couple years, most firms will grant four weeks, and eventually move you up to six weeks. However, at that point, you'll be close to partner level, and unlikely be able to spare the additional time away from the firm.

Most firms understand how demanding the job can be, and they know that, ideally, you should get some good time each year to decompress.

Actually scheduling a vacation is another story. Consulting projects can have a life of their own, and project managers need key resources when you least expect it. Planning a vacation on short notice usually won't work, because your project manager needs time to fill your spot while you are gone. If you want to take a vacation in the consulting industry, you need to plan it far in advance and remind people of your approaching vacation to avoid any confusion. It's a good idea to start every project communicating everyone's "blackout days" to each other and agreeing to adhere to them as best as possible.

Even so, there are plenty of stories of consultants whose vacation was delayed, shortened or flat out cancelled due to project needs. Some firms will reimburse you for the resulting costs incurred, and others will just expect you to take the sacrifice in stride—this is just one of many areas where firm culture becomes extremely important to your ability to enjoy your job. Regarding the quality of your vacation when you do take it: If you are playing a key role in a project, you should expect to take your laptop, stay online, keep your cell phone on while you're away and be receptive to adjusting your activities around some bits of work here and there. "Going black" (being off e-mail and voice mail—say, for example, by going camping in the mountains, or staying at a cheap hotel without Wi-Fi) during a vacation is not advisable unless it's clear that there's no possible way you could be needed, and you are confident that you've built up enough of a good reputation to not seem like a slacker.

Work hard, play hard

Reputable firms spare no expense for the hardworking employees who drive their revenue growth. Consulting is all about working hard and playing hard, and consultants play very hard.

That said, your project's entertainment budget will depend on how much work your partners sell, the price of the work and the negotiating skills of your partners. Generally, you can tell how big the fun budget will be by the type of client. Government clients aren't big spenders. Expect the project dinners to be middle-of-the-road, infrequent and no fun. Work in financial services or pharmaceuticals, however, and the budgets are much better, sometimes lavish. But don't worry too much about the project budgets. If your project doesn't have a lot of fun money, your firm often chips in for your enjoyment.

Consulting firms are, by and large, very friendly places where people form long-lasting relationships. Partying with your peers and colleagues is all part of the experience, and consultants (partners included) party a lot. Join a consulting firm and you will reap the social perks. Just remember to take a breather from time to time, because too many nights with just four hours of sleep will take their toll.

Maintaining a personal life from afar

Many new consultants are not prepared for the difficulty of maintaining friendships and personal relationships from the road. You vow to stay in touch with your friends, but then you find yourself exhausted on the weekends and unable to schedule time for a personal call to a friend during the week. As a result, you can lose touch with your friends. Moreover, it can be very hard to maintain a relationship with a significant other, let alone a family, when you are away from home three nights a week.

That said, if you are going to make this career work for you, you will need to take responsibility for keeping close to loved ones. While consulting has its unexpected crises, the schedule can be predictable. So plan ahead!

- Every Monday, for example, schedule what fun or intimate event you are going to have with your spouse, significant other or family. Also on Monday, pick one or two friends and call them that evening to make plans for Thursday, Friday or Saturday, whatever you have available.

- You might want to consider setting up a standing appointment with a set of friends, to make sure you keep in touch. How about meeting with your closest friends every third Sunday of the month for brunch?

- Also, if you haven't already, get used to relying on your cell phone as your true source of connection with others. Perhaps you have lots of friends that you want to stay in touch with, or you prioritize speaking with your family every day. Carve out bits of time here and there to call them on your cell phone. Good times include: in the car driving to and from the client, during lunch or right after dinner. Remember that you only need 10 minutes to speak with people. During the next flight delay you have, make your calls.

- Another lifesaver is online bill payment services. Check with your bank to see if you can automate as many monthly bills as possible. This will allow you to spend less time on the weekends doing paperwork and more time with the people in your life.

- Need balance? Why not sign up for a weekend art or music program? Maybe you can attend a weekend class at a local institution.

Sounds too regimented? Take it from a few current and former consultants—it is all too easy to let life slip away. A happy, fulfilling personal life makes a happy consultant.

Diversity Issues in Consulting: State of the Industry

Cultural and gender diversity continues to increase in management consulting firms, just as in other areas of the business world. At the same time, many people point out that the diversity tends to be visual in nature—how much diversity of ideas are we really achieving?

Didn't I see you at the polo match last weekend?

Consulting is not so different from other business jobs, in that people tend to hire people who are like themselves. This phenomenon is exacerbated by the "fit" interview approach that dominates consulting. Most well-educated, intelligent people who prepare a bit can solve case interview questions adequately, at which point the hiring process comes down to the subjective assessment of "fit." As a result, the character of the consulting workforce is painfully slow to change over time, and there's little room for employees who fall too far from the tree on any given dimension. Consulting firms can point to having made some important (though insufficient) strides in getting their numbers of ethnic minorities and women up, but they have a harder time pointing to diversity in academic background, life experience or socio-economic status. In addition, one area where many consulting firms (and much of the business world in general) have been less progressive is in providing welcoming environments for openly gay and lesbian employees—there still is not enough social pressure for these firms to feel compelled to foster and then tout an explicitly gay-friendly environment.

Here's the bottom line: It's a well-known phenomenon that, walking through the halls of a name brand firm, you are likely to see a group that is thinner, taller, more athletic, whiter, more male and blonder than the U.S. population as a whole. Though it's less obvious to the casual observer, job candidates quickly discover a uniformity in personality as well. This is not as controversial a statement as you might think. One top-five MBA program has all of its matriculating students take the Meyers-Briggs personality type indicator test, and keeps track of aggregate stats over the years. The school reports that, while the U.S. population is fairly evenly distributed over the 16 distinct personality types identified by Meyers and Briggs, fully 75 percent of their MBA graduates turn out to be one of just two personality types! (ENTP and ENTJ, if you're curious.) Consequently, management consulting firms (which are for the most part composed of MBAs) wind up one-dimensional in terms of personality—a characteristic that reflects the applicant pool more than anything.

Even early in their careers, consultants have high-profile roles selling and presenting to very senior, illustrious executives. It's understandable that employers seek to fill that role with charismatic, approachable, articulate, visually pleasing people. Yet the figurative "beauty contest" element of consulting recruiting limits the progress in achieving true diversity. It's important to truly fit in to a firm's culture to get hired in the first place, and subsequently to maintain your job.

- We know of one mainstream U.S. firm, for example, that was founded by a native of India; despite having grown into a top-20 sized firm, its Indian employees are overrepresented relative to the U.S. population by nearly 10 times, and most of them are from one particular Indian ethnic group to boot. Consultants report that this fairly large firm has no openly gay employees, no women partners and no working mothers.

- Another consulting firm was founded by science PhDs from a leading research university. The firm now hires a mixture of MBAs, PhDs and quantitatively-oriented BAs, and is known for having a friendly yet nerdy culture. That firm has but one female partner among dozens, and just two post-MBA female consultants—yet is progressive in offering generous flex-time, embracing openly gay employees and employing a healthy mix of ethnic minorities. Does this situation reflect self-selection in the applicant pool? Or does the interviewer pool subconsciously gravitate to applicants like themselves, keeping the gender mix static?

The bottom line is that if you want to work and succeed in consulting, realistically you need to slot right into the existing environment, not hope to be the first of a wave of new blood that ultimately changes that environment. Tried-and-true fit interview techniques are just as important to master as your case frameworks: Mirror the interviewer's body language, tone and pace of speaking, level of seriousness and overall demeanor. Learn to play golf or tennis, be conversant in the latest business and sports news, know your wines and single-malts, and seem decently well-traveled and well-read. All of these things will help get you hired, and then help you stay on the job over the long term.

That said, the narrowly-defined fit mold is far more marked among the large, well-known global strategy firms—which means that, on the flip side, the smaller, lower-profile firms (e.g., many of the specialty boutiques we profiled earlier) may present better odds if you somehow don't fit the prototypical consultant mold.

Mommy-tracking, even if you're not a mommy

The problems faced by women in consulting have been particularly slow to see improvement. Many firms now have marquee programs to attract and retain women—yet one wonders how much is PR versus real effort to make a difference. The numbers still reveal that most firms have painfully few women partners and senior managers (or they have a few senior women in roles like HR and marketing). Despite the ongoing "opt out" versus "pushed out" debate in the media, it seems clear that the consulting world has been guilty of the latter. Women still bear the brunt of child care and elder care in our society, and given that the traditional consulting schedule is incompatible with family obligations for all but the very wealthy, women end up forced out or backed into such corners that they leave "voluntarily" for more flexible positions.

Firms vary dramatically in the benefits and flexibility offered to parents. One litigation support boutique refuses to provide a lactation room, resulting in the humiliation of women pumping as they hunch behind their desks in glass offices. At the same time, one large strategy firm offers on-site subsidized day care and no-strings-attached flex-time during the day to meet last-minute family obligations. If these issues matter to you, you should feel very comfortable asking about a firm's policies up front in the interview process. Getting hired by a firm that simply won't accommodate your personal situation will only hold back your career in the long run, compared to finding a good fit from the get-go.

But being a mother is not the only issue that holds women back—it's also just being female. Consulting firm management teams remain old boys' clubs to a great extent. Stories abound of women who thought they were doing good work, received good performance reviews and got accolades from clients, but were dismissed without cause anyway. This is an unfortunate reality for women at the senior associate/manager level and above—at the business analyst level, most management consultancies with any critical mass have achieved and are able to maintain a 50/50 gender ratio.

Gender discrimination lawsuits are sadly still fairly frequent in the management consulting world—few of them, of course, make the press due to being settled before they reach the courts. We've heard firsthand reports of recent situations in well-regarded firms where women felt they were dismissed after complaining about sexual harassment, not hired in the first place because their age implied they might be a "baby risk," or asked to resign after rubbing the (male) team the wrong way by not joining in on baseball talk and after-work baseball games. At the end of the day, nobody likes the odd person out, and women still often find themselves to be one of few in a given situation in the consulting world.

It boils down again to "fit"—if you don't have that certain something, no amount of clever Excel modeling and creative PowerPoint structuring can overcome the subconscious issue a male supervisor may have with you. There's not much you can do to mitigate this reality, apart from seeking out firms whose management team composition appears to reflect a willingness to accept women into the leadership fold, and then putting your head down and forging ahead with your best work.

Days in the Life
CHAPTER 11

It's tough to visualize yourself as a consultant if you haven't been there and done that. Here, we bring you real days in the life of consultants at different levels and at different types of consulting firms. Is this lifestyle for you?

Associate

Greg Schneider is an associate at the Boston office of a top strategy consulting firm. He kindly agreed to share a "typical" workday with Vault, noting that no day at any consulting firm can be called typical.

6:15 a.m.: Alarm goes off. I wake up asking myself why I put "run three times per week" into the team charter. I meet another member of the team, and we hobble out for a jog. At least it's warm out—another advantage of having a project in Miami.

7:15 a.m.: Check voice mail. Someone in London wants a copy of my knowledge-building document on managing hypergrowth. A co-worker is looking for information about what it's like to work with the partner from my last team.

7:30 a.m.: Breakfast with the team. We discuss sports, *Letterman* and a morning meeting we have with the client team (not necessarily in that order). We then head out to the client.

9:00 a.m.: Meet with the client team. We've got an important progress review with the CEO next week, so there's a lot going on. We're helping the client to assess the market potential of an emerging technology. Today's meeting concerns what kind of presentation would be most effective, although we have trouble staying off tangents about the various analyses that we've all been working on. The discussion is complicated by the fact that some key data is not yet available. We elect to go with a computer-based slide show and begin the debate on content.

10:53 a.m.: Check voice mail. The office is looking for an interviewer for the Harvard Business School hell weekend. The partner will be arriving in time for dinner and wants to meet to discuss the progress review. A headhunter looking for a divisional VP. My wife reminding me to mail off the insurance forms.

11:00 a.m.: I depart with my teammate for an interview. We meet with an industry expert (a professor from a local university) to discuss industry trends and, in particular, what the prospects are for the type of technology we're looking at. As this is the last interview we plan to do, we are able to check many of our hypotheses. The woman is amazing—we luck out and get some data that we need. The bad news is, now we have to figure out what it means.

12:28 p.m.: As I walk back in to the client, a division head I've been working with grabs me and we head to lunch. He wanted to discuss an analysis he'd given me some information for, and in the process I get some interesting perspectives about the difficulties in moving the technology into full production and how much it could cost.

1:30 p.m.: I jump on a quick conference call about an internal knowledge-building project I'm working on for the marketing practice. I successfully avoid taking on any additional responsibility.

2:04 p.m.: Begin to work through new data. After discussing the plan of attack with the engagement manager, I dive in. It's a very busy afternoon, but the data is great. I get a couple "a-ha"s—always a good feeling.

3:00 p.m.: Short call with someone from Legal to get an update on the patent search.

6:00 p.m.: Team meeting. The engagement manager pulls the team together to check progress on various fronts and debate some issues prior to heading to dinner with the partner. A quick poll determines that Italian food wins—we leave a voice mail with the details.

6:35 p.m.: Call home and check in with the family. Confirm plans for weekend trip to Vermont. Apologize for forgetting to mail the insurance forms.

7:15 p.m.: The team packs up and heads out to dinner. We meet the partner at the restaurant and have a productive (and caloric) meal working through our plans for the progress review, the new data, what's going on with the client team and other areas of interest. She suggests some additional uses for the new data, adds her take on our debates and agrees to raise a couple issues with the CFO, whom she's known for years. She takes a copy of our draft presentation to read after dinner.

9:15 p.m.: Return to hotel. Plug in computer and check e-mail, since I hadn't had a chance all day. While I'm logged in, I download two documents I need from the company database, check the Red Sox score, and see how the client's stock did.

10:10 p.m.: Pre-sleep voice mail check. A client from a previous study is looking for one of the appendices, since he lost his copy. The server will be down for an hour tomorrow night.

10:30 p.m.: Watch *SportsCenter* instead of going right to sleep, as I know I probably should.

Note: Had this been an in-town study, the following things would have been different: I wouldn't have run with another member of my team, and we'd have substituted a conference call for the dinner meeting, so we could go home instead. Also, I probably wouldn't have watched *SportsCenter*.

Consultant Project Manager

Hans Helbekkmo is a project manager. He kindly agreed to share a "typical" workday with Vault.

6:00 a.m.: Alarm goes off, Monday morning. I take a few seconds to remember that I'm in Lyon, where I've just spent a terrific weekend with my girlfriend. I have to catch a 8:30 flight to Düsseldorf, where I've been working on a project for the past five months.

8:15 a.m.: After checking in, I phone up my team and tell them I'll be in around 10. Richard, a first-year consultant, tells me that Jason, the director primarily responsible for the project, left a message that he wanted to see the presentation document for our afternoon meeting with the client board member in charge of our workstream [in planning our schedule]. Otherwise no important messages. I check my voicemail messages and learn that Jason, just returned from holiday, was unaware of our meeting, but he can make it.

9:30 a.m.: Land in Düsseldorf and jump in a cab. While our project requires that we spend at least Monday through Thursday on the client site, I pretty much spend every weekend out of town, either at home in New York, traveling to visit friends or family, or simply finding a spot on the map with better weather than the Ruhrgebiet [the Ruhr Valley]. My company covers reasonable travel expenses, which makes life more enjoyable. And I'm now an expert on finding the fastest route through customs/immigration and getting to the front of the taxi queue in zero time.

10:00 a.m.: Arrive at work. Jason's already in and is discussing the presentation document with Daniel, the other consultant on my team. Jason tells me that Gerhard, the director responsible for the overall client relationship, cannot make the afternoon meeting. Not a disaster—it is very hard to schedule meetings with a board-level client, and I'm perfectly happy bringing just one director along.

10:15 a.m.: I change into a suit and catch up on the conversation. Jason is happy with what we've put together, but he has some detailed questions on a couple of our charts. Daniel shows us an alternative analysis that makes the same points more convincingly. We decide to go with the new slides, and cut down the document a bit to keep it "short and sweet."

10:30 a.m.: Finally time to check my e-mail. I have about 20 new messages, mostly personal or process-related. A colleague wants to pick my brains on asset/liability management and liquidity management. Gerhard says he wants to discuss Daniel's midyear review, so I put this into my "to-do" list.

Richard already had his review on Friday, so I make a note of talking to him about it later.

11:00 a.m.: While Daniel is working on the document changes, I go through an outline for our final presentation with Jason. We have less than one month left, and I want to get Jason's input. We are working toward a quite comprehensive strategic review. It is very clear what the right solution for the bank is, but we need to put together a detailed explanation of the implications and likely outcomes, so our client can convince the full board to approve our proposed initiatives. Jason agrees with the main contents and level of detail, and he does not have any further suggestions.

Directors typically give the project team full responsibility for developing recommendations and executing the project on a day-to-day basis, which makes my job both challenging and rewarding. We will have a more detailed review once all the interviews and analysis are done and the final document is drafted. For now I just want to make sure we're all on the same track.

12:00 p.m.: Time for lunch—Jason and Daniel decide to grab a sandwich, so I take Richard to the Italian cafe across the street. I ask how his midyear review went, and he say he's happy with it—no surprises, nothing new was mentioned that I hadn't already discussed with him. He was told to focus on improving his communication and process skills. Richard has a PhD in finance and has just started working for us. I tell him it is typical for someone who's worked in academia for a while to need some time to adjust to the particular demands of our job in terms of client communication. It is sometimes difficult to adapt to the comprehension level of our clients, especially since we tend to have a very strong analytical and theoretical knowledge base, while our clients have a much more practical background.

In any case, I'm happy that Richard agrees with our assessment of his performance.

1:00 p.m.: I sit down with Richard to get an update on the database work he's been doing over the past couple of days. We're broadly on track, though we need to get a couple of extra data fields to produce the reports we want to deliver. I ask him to discuss this with the client's systems people and try to find a solution that doesn't produce undue additional workload. We only have a couple of weeks to get the reporting up and running, so I'm a bit worried about our progress. The systems people have been predictably slow in providing us with data, so the result is likely to be some late hours next week. That's the nature of this job—when things go as planned, we rarely do more than 50 to 55 hours a week, but the occasional crunch or hiccup from the client can easily result in 18-hour days. Our company is strongly committed to avoiding long hours, and it is largely my responsibility to make sure this is complied with. This requires careful planning and occasionally standing my ground with clients and project directors, making sure not to commit to unreasonable deliverables.

2:00 p.m.: Jean-Pierre, our main day-to-day client contact, phones me to make sure we're on track for the meeting. I confirm that everything's fine and that we should meet outside the client's office at 5:30. I mail him the latest version of the document.

2:30 p.m.: Daniel has finished the edits. We go through the document one last time. It's a convincing "story" and has the right level of detail.

3:00 p.m.: Jason and I sit down to plan the meeting. The board-level client is likely to have about 45 minutes, and he probably won't have many questions. We decide not to draw too many conclusions when discussing the slides, but rather try to invite discussion and get a sense of where he wants to go with this. The topics we're dealing with have strong political implications, and we need to trust his judgement on how aggressively we should formulate our recommendations. After all, it is our main job to provide content and insight, while the client really remains the expert on internal politics.

3:45 p.m.: I phone up my travel agent to confirm my trip to New York next weekend.

5:15 p.m.: Jason and I discuss whether we should bring Richard and Daniel to the meeting. We usually involve junior staff in as many discussions as possible and give them an opportunity to present their own results. However, the meeting is likely to be conducted in German, which would leave Daniel stranded, so we decide not to bring them along.

5:30 p.m.: Jason and I meet up with Jean-Pierre, and the meeting starts on time. I quickly talk the board-level client through the document—in English after all. He agrees with the main messages and says we should state our findings and recommendations very clearly, although this may upset some of the other board members. He says he will try to get a decision on our strategy within two months.

6:15 p.m.: Quick debrief with Jean-Pierre and Jason.

6:30 p.m.: I summarize the meeting for Daniel and Richard and give them due credit for their good work.

7:00 p.m.: Jason jumps on a train back to Frankfurt, and I take my team out for dinner. Düsseldorf has a large selection of terrific Japanese restaurants, and we pick our favorite to celebrate a successful day. The conversation meanders through the Mexican election, U.S. drug policy, quantum computers and the latest Nick Hornby novel. Shop talk is strictly off-limits during evenings, a policy I've adapted from my previous job managers.

10:00 p.m.: We move on to the Altstadt for a few drinks.

11:00 p.m.: I go home to my flat, watch the last half-hour of *Poltergeist* in German, read another chapter of *The Name of The Rose*, where Adso spends five pages musing on the religious justification for his sinful desires—which finally puts me to sleep.

MBA-level Strategy Consultant

Dan is a 28-year-old recent graduate of a top business school. Dan lives in Boston and works for a firm generally regarded as one of the top strategic consultancies worldwide. Before business school, Dan worked in operations management for a large health care provider. Presently, Dan resides in Boston and works in the pharmaceutical industry group at the firm.

5:45 a.m.: The alarm clock rings—it's Monday morning, and I instantly calculate the amount of time I have to get to the airport. I have a very important client meeting at 1 p.m. near Cleveland, and a 7:30 a.m. departure. Airport security delays [post 9/11] have been terrible, so I have to allow more time.

6:10 a.m.: Checking e-mail from my laptop dial-up connection while shaving, I look through an e-mail from Rolph, my engagement manager at ABC Pharmaceuticals in Cleveland. The request is for clarification on a section of the financial model I created over the weekend. While packing my suitcase, I dash off a few sentences to explain key assumptions in the statement of cash flows. The e-mail only takes a few minutes, but I'm worried it could make me miss my flight.

6:28 a.m.: I get on the T [Boston's subway system] for what's normally a 35-minute ride to Logan airport from my Back Bay apartment. Normally, a taxi ride would be better since I could open up my laptop and do some work, but I have learned from hard experience that the potential variance on traffic jams is just too risky. The T is a little slower, but a lot more predictable. I get a cup of coffee from an underground vendor just as the trolley car pulls in to the Marlborough station.

6:57 a.m.: The T pulls up to the transfer stop—I scurry onto the shuttle bus for the 10-minute transfer to Terminal A. I'm really cutting it close. Above ground again off the subway, I check my cell phone voice mail—seven messages this morning. That's not too bad for a Monday morning.

7:05 a.m.: Rushing into Terminal A, I make a beeline to American's self check-in station. You must always use the self check-in station.

7:16 a.m.: Whew—close one. Running up to Gate 47, I was distressed to see how eerily quiet the gate area was. Luckily, a flight attendant saw my frantic waving and kept the door open a few moments longer.

7:45 a.m.: Airborne after a slight air traffic delay, I seize a chance to crack open the laptop. Time to get focused on the day's work. I spend the body of the 90-minute flight toggling back and forth on the pivot table in the Excel model—making changes to help clarify the statement of cash flows and head off potential ambiguities.

9:15 a.m.: "We are beginning our initial descent into the Cleveland area." I wrap up my work and take a few moments to check my car rental reservations and confirm my schedule for the rest of the day. Unfortunately, since the client headquarters is in a far-off suburb of Cleveland, a taxi trip is not an option. I count back the minutes from 1 p.m. With luck, I can be at the client site by 11 a.m. Just getting to the car rental pickup location could easily take 45 minutes.

9:57 a.m.: On the car rental shuttle bus with my early-morning adrenaline wearing off, I feel drowsy. Eyes shut, I ponder my decision to go home over the past weekend. My two colleagues on the engagement, Rolph and Jorge, elected to stay at the client site to work through the weekend. I went home, but now I'm regretting my decision.

10:12 a.m.: Finally on the road to ABC Pharmaceuticals after a quick car pickup at National's Emerald Aisle.

11:07 a.m.: Almost five hours after leaving home, I walk into conference room 52 A, the temporary location I have occupied for the past few weeks. In the corner, Jorge, the BA-level research analyst assigned to this project, is typing feverishly on his computer—he doesn't even notice me enter.

Logging in to the client's network, I see to my dismay that 23 new e-mails have materialized. From the number of messages with "urgent" in the subject line, I gather that the morning has not gone well.

11:12 a.m.: Finally getting Jorge's attention and asking where Rolph is, I learn that Rolph has spent the morning shuttling from client manager to client manager, attempting to keep the project on track. Apparently, last week, M&A rumors surfaced in the industry, and now key managers in the operating division were questioning whether the organizational restructuring that we're working on is part of a broader plan to spin off the business unit.

11:17 a.m.: Still wondering where Rolph is, I open up the 58-slide PowerPoint presentation that they are set to review at 1 p.m. to begin making final edits and incorporating the updated Excel spreadsheets.

11:20 a.m.: Moments later, Rolph strides in, looking exasperated. "We need a major overhaul," he announces. Jorge and I exchange glances. "The division VP has had a change of heart—we need to adjust the restructuring plan." Listening intently as Rolph recaps the dozen conversations he's had throughout the morning, I flip through the PowerPoint deck, reviewing the major sections and content of individual slides. Suddenly, an idea hits me. I outline a plan to revise the presentation, adding a brief new section in the beginning and moving most of the main body of the presentation to an appendix in the back. "Just what I was thinking," Rolph nods.

11:30 a.m.: Having divided the 58 slides into three parts, Rolph, Jorge and I "divide and conquer" to plow through the modifications they discussed. I take the largest section of slides—30 in total, and am proud to set a pace of three minutes per slide for modifications.

1:00 p.m.: The 90 minutes have flown by, but the pieces are coming together. Rolph and Jorge are already in the meeting room, getting things started and passing out agendas. I cut and paste the last section of slides into my master deck. I send the deck to the assigned executive assistant for printing and photocopying.

1:15 p.m.: I step into the conference room, joining Rolph at the head of the table with the 15 client managers seated before them. Rolph has been in front of the group for 10 minutes, giving an overview of current status and buying time. I plug my laptop into the overhead projector just as the assistant distributes the photocopied handouts to the group.

1:17 p.m.: Stepping to the front of the room, I start my detailed discussion of the presentation slides. Dan is the primary "owner" of the deliverable. As the consultant who translates Rolph's direction into action and the person who directs Jorge's efforts—I am the "point person" for changes to the actual deliverable.

1:23 p.m.: Six minutes into my presentation, the first client manager interrupts to question the deliverable.

1:37 p.m.: Pushing through the presentation with a detailed knowledge of the material and client facilitation skills learned in the past few months, the meeting finally bogs down—what was intended as a "summary of deliverable" meeting has become a highly contentious work session. Faced with an increasing pace of client objections and new client information, I can only look to Rolph.

1:38 p.m.: Recognizing the changed climate of the meeting, Rolph steps to the front to relieve me. After directing Jorge to grab a flip chart from the room next door, Rolph scrawls a new agenda with a magic marker.

3:55 p.m.: By now, all participants in the room realize that the entire scope of the project has changed—not just the specifics of the deliverable, but the project objectives, stakeholders, structure and timetable. I discretely open my Palm Pilot to begin to identify the ripple effect on my schedule for the rest of the week. No major crisis points, fortunately—but he will need to get in touch with the manager for my other project in Atlanta ASAP. It looks like I will be in Cleveland for at least another two days this week.

4:15 p.m.: The meeting concludes, and Rolph, Jorge and I quickly excuse ourselves to check messages on e-mail and voice mail.

4:20 p.m.: I get on the phone with the firm's travel desk, canceling the flight to Atlanta tonight and rescheduling for Thursday.

4:30 p.m.: I e-mail the Atlanta project manager, explaining the changes to the Cleveland project and requesting advice on next steps. I then e-mail the firm's Research Network in Washington, following up on an earlier request for a dedicated researcher to analyze a client's survey results. I also send about a dozen other e-mails to colleagues to coordinate on other matters.

4:40 p.m.: Back in conference room 52A, Jorge is already typing up output from Rolph's flip charts. The next two hours are spent reviewing the outcome of the meeting, discussing necessary changes to the project timeline and deliverables and prioritizing next steps.

5:30 p.m.: Rolph suggests ordering some food. He needs to get to the airport for a flight to New York, to assist a partner on a business development proposal with a financial services firm located there. The first real meal of the day arrives at about 6:15 p.m.—I pick at the lo mein absently as I stare at the financial model on my laptop.

7:30 p.m.: Feeling like the pharmaceutical client project's deliverables are under control for the time being, I check e-mail again and messages again—several administrative items have popped up over the weekend and during the day. Having previously ignored them, I open up the messages partially for the relief of looking at something new. There's a request for feedback on my last project—an opportunity to provide 360 degree (upward) feedback on my last project manager. There is a reply from the Research Network group, providing a choice of several assistants for the Atlanta project. There is also an e-mail from the SCG travel desk, confirming travel reservations for later in the week.

9:00 p.m.: Jorge gets up to pack up the laptop and go back to the hotel. Jorge and I chat briefly about the weekend and the hotel Rolph and Jorge are both staying at. I keep working, now turning my attention to reviewing data and project materials for the Atlanta project.

9:30 p.m.: The cleaning crew stops by, emptying the wastebaskets and spraying Lysol on the desks. I get a headache but continue to work.

10:15 p.m.: Feeling very tired now, I opt to pack it in. I get the rental car, and drive the five miles to the hotel.

11:00 p.m.: I call my girlfriend, set the alarm for 6:00 a.m. tomorrow and go to sleep.

IT Strategy Consultant

Kristine is a consultant at a major consulting firm with many IT consulting engagements. She graduated with a BA in business administration and has been with the company for four years. She's recently been staffed at a large telecommunications company. The company is revamping sales training. Her role is team lead of the design and developer for eight web-based training modules. She has five analysts on her team.

4:30 a.m.: It's Monday morning. Time to wake up. There's time for a shower this Monday morning—such luxury!

5:30 a.m.: I am in a cab on the way to the airport, making a mental list of anything that could have been forgotten. I ask the cabbie to tune the radio to NPR.

6:10 a.m.: At the airport I go up to the self check-in kiosk. I take the boarding pass and head down to the security line, laptop and small carry-on in hand.

6:25 a.m.: At security, I remove my laptop from my bag and place it on the tray. I move through security quickly. No alarms beep.

6:35 a.m.: After a quick stop at Starbucks, I arrive at the gate. I say hello to three other members of my project and check out the other passengers I see every week on this Monday morning flight. I board early along with the other premier fliers—one of the perks of being a frequent traveler.

7:00 a.m.: The flight departs on time. Yay! I relish my window seat close to the front of the airplane.

8:00 a.m.: The beverage cart wakes me up. I ask for coffee and scan *The Wall Street Journal* as I drink.

9:30 a.m.: I arrive at my destination and share a ride with my fellow consultants to the project site.

10:30 a.m.: At the project site. As I crawl underneath my desk to hook my laptop to the client LAN connection, one of my team members informs me that he still hasn't received feedback from his client reviewer. That's not good news.

11:00 a.m.: After checking and responding to e-mail, I call my team member's client reviewer. The reviewer agrees to send me the team member feedback on the training material by noon tomorrow.

11:15 a.m.: I remind the team of the 1 p.m. status meeting. I've got to start it on time—I have a meeting downtown at 3:15 p.m. I start to review the content outlines for the training modules.

12:00 p.m.: I scurry, along with two teammates, to get sandwiches at a nearby eatery. Mine is turkey and cheddar.

12:20 p.m.: Back at my desk, I get a call from the project manager, who is working at a client site in another state. He tells me that clients in the training department are nervous about their job security and asks that the entire team be sensitive to how the training changes may affect the training positions in the organization.

1:00 p.m.: The team holds a status meeting. I pass on the message from the project manager. Each member discusses what has been completed and what he or she expects to complete that week. Two other team members are having difficulty obtaining feedback from their client reviewers. We all brainstorm on how to obtain the feedback.

2:00 p.m.: I finish up the meeting and get directions to my meeting downtown.

2:40 p.m.: Off to the 3:15 p.m. meeting.

3:15 p.m.: I meet the head of the training department to discuss the training courses. He calls in a close associate who has opinions on how the courses should be organized. The associate wants to add several more web-based training modules. I politely suggest that part of the additional subject matter could be covered in the modules that have been agreed to in the scope of the project. We all sketch out the course structure on a white board.

4:45 p.m.: Back at the project site. I check in with my team members via e-mail.

5:45 p.m.: I complete a draft of the course flow in PowerPoint and send it to the client and my manager for review.

7:00 p.m.: I have reviewed 50 percent of the course outlines. It's time to head back to the hotel. I stop by a local diner for a quick dinner.

8:30 p.m.: Time for a workout in the hotel gym.

9:15 p.m.: I'm ready for bed. Clothes for the next day are hanging in the closet. The alarm clock is set to 6:30 a.m.

10:30 p.m.: I go to sleep.

Conclusion

Management consulting can involve demanding, long hours. The travel can wear you down. The pressure of producing top-notch, error-free deliverables within a short period of time can be grueling. And it's a notoriously difficult field to get into. On the other hand, you can gain an incredible amount of general business, analytical, and industry knowledge in just a few years—likely more than you could in any other field. As a consultant, you will work with some extremely bright, inquisitive, and energetic colleagues. The salary and benefits are generous relative to many other business jobs. And with the right role, you can position yourself well for graduate school or your next career move.

These pros and cons trade off differently for different people, which is to say that consulting certainly isn't for everyone. Our suggestion is that if you're on the fence about joining the world of consulting, err on the side of going for it. Consulting jobs open up lots of doors for post-consulting jobs, positioning you powerfully to go after another job that you desperately want later on.

The application process turns out to be a great way to learn about the career path itself, so you'll have more clarity about your interest level in consulting once you actually have a job offer in front of you. After going through the recruiting process, the worst case scenario is that you don't find a position that fits you, but you've spent some valuable hours practicing case interviews with frameworks that will serve you well in your business career. At best, you find yourself with a fulfilling, exciting job that could last you many years.

We hope this guidebook becomes a well-worn resource in your briefcase, by your nightstand, and possibly in your Tuesday night hotel room as you make your way through the sometimes crazy but rewarding career that is management consulting. Enjoy the ride!

Get the BUZZ on Top Schools

Read what **STUDENTS** and **ALUMNI** have to say about:

- Admissions
- Academics
- Career Opportunities
- Quality of Life
- Social Life

Surveys on thousands of top programs
College • MBA • Law School • Grad School

VAULT
> the most trusted name in career information™

Go to www.vault.com

APPENDIX

Industry Buzzwords

The consulting industry uses many buzzwords. Consultants easily lapse into their lingo while conversing with the layman, imposing panic on those who were unaware they even possess a "skill set" (those areas where you excel). Here is a short rundown of some of those words that consultants like to throw around:

APD: Advanced professional degree (e.g., JD, PhD or MD).

Application service provider (ASP): A company that offers its clients online access to applications that would otherwise be located in their own computers.

B2B: Business-to-business.

B2C: Business-to-consumer.

Balanced scorecard: A conceptual framework for translating an organization's vision into a set of performance indicators distributed among four perspectives: financial, customer, internal business processes, and learning and growth.

Bananagram: A graph showing profitability vs. relative market share. The graph shows that the higher the market share, the higher the profitability. (The typical measure of profitability for this graph is return on capital employed, or "ROCE" [pronounced "roachy"].)

BCG matrix: A portfolio assessment tool developed by The Boston Consulting Group. Also called a growth-share matrix.

Benchmarking: Measuring a value, practice or other quantity (such as costs) against those of other companies in the industry.

Blank slide: Initial sketch on paper for a slide to be used in a case presentation (called blank because it does not include data until analysts input it).

Brainteaser: A consulting interview question in which the job seeker is asked to solve a logic problem.

Boiling the ocean: When a project team finds itself faced with an impossibly large amount of data.

Business process reengineering (BPR): The process of reviewing a client's business processes, eliminating unneeded or "nonvalue-added" tasks, and then implementing the leaner, more efficient process.

Case team: A team working on a consulting project for a client; usually composed of one partner (or director), one consultant and two or more analysts.

Change management: A service where the firm helps a company cope with a period of significant change (such as a merger, downsizing or restructuring).

Consultancy: A typically European term for "consulting firm," though the word has picked up currency in the United States.

Core competencies: The areas in which a company excels. Consultants believe a company should enter only those businesses that are part of its core competencies.

Critical path: A term from operations management theory. Every business process consists of a series of tasks. Some of these tasks are related to maintenance of the process or administrative and bookkeeping issues. Taken away, they do not directly impact the end result of the business process. If you eliminate these tasks, there remains the core set of tasks that must occur in order to produce the desired result. This is the critical path. In everyday consulting language, the term refers to only those work tasks that are most important at the time.

Customer relationship management (CRM): A term that refers to the data-gathering methods used to collect information about a client's customers. CRM usually focuses on sales force automation, customer service/call center, field service and marketing automation.

DCF: Discounted cash flow. The present value of a future cash flow.

Deck: A report detailing client issues and recommendations from the project team. Also known as a "deliverable."

Drilldown: Asking questions to gather more detail about a situation, usually from a high-level (big-picture) view.

80/20 rule: Getting 80 percent of the answer in 20 percent of your time. The other 80 percent of your time might not be worth it. (A favorite of Bain Chairman Orit Gadiesh.)

Engagement: A consulting assignment received by a consulting firm; also called a "case" or "project."

Enterprise resource planning (ERP): Processes or software that help streamline departments or divisions of a company.

Experience curve: The principle that a company's cost declines as its production increases. One assumption used by consultants is that a company's costs decline by roughly 25 percent for every doubling in production (e.g., a company's 200th unit of a product costs 75 percent of the 100th unit's cost).

Granularity: Refers to the basic elements that make up a business problem. Imagine a handful of sand. At a high level, it is simply a handful of sand. At a granular level, it is bits of rock and shell matter reduced to fine granules over time by the ocean.

Guesstimate: A type of consulting interview question. Guesstimates require job seekers to make an educated estimate of something (often the size of the market for a particular product or service) using basic calculations.

High-level view: Also referred to as a "50,000-foot view." It describes a situation in general terms or as an overview of a situation. Also known as "helicoptering."

Hoteling/hot desking: A system used to assign space to consultants working on site. Consultants move around so much that in some firms they are not assigned permanent offices—just a voice mail extension. Whenever they know they need to work on site, they call up the office nearest them to request a desk.

Hurdle rate: A company's cost of capital. In general, if the return on an investment exceeds the hurdle rate, the company should make the investment.

Implementation: The process by which a consulting firm ensures that the advice it gives to a client company is enacted.

Incubator: A place or situation that encourages the formation and development of new companies by providing certain services (e.g., office space, Internet connections, support staff).

Learning curve: The rate at which a consultant acquires background information or industry knowledge needed for a case. A steep curve is a good thing.

Letter of engagement (LOE)/letter of intent (LOI)/letter of proposal (LOP): A sales pitch to a potential client that lays out how and on what a consulting team will focus its efforts and what results the client should expect.

Net present value: The sum of a series of discounted cash flows. This is the most common metric used to assess the profitability for a client of making an investment or undertaking a project.

O'Hare test: A test used by interviewers to assess personality fit. "If I were stuck overnight with this person at O'Hare Airport, would I have fun?"

On the beach: The time between assignments, when consultants' work hours usually decline significantly. This expression originated at McKinsey.

Out-of-the-box thinking: Creativity.

Outsourcing: Hiring an outside vendor to perform a task normally performed within a company, often at a lower cost and with better results. Examples of processes commonly outsourced include payroll, data processing, recruitment, accounting and document processing.

Pigeonholing: Usually refers to a consultant's becoming overspecialized.

Porter, Michael: A founding principal of Monitor Group and the father of the consulting framework known as Porter's Five Forces.

Reengineering: A largely discredited fad of the early 1990s, which advocates a complete overhaul (and usually downsizing) of a company's strategies, operations and practices.

Rightsizing: Also known as "downsizing"—just a kinder, gentler term for restructuring the elements of a company. This is most often used in reference to headcount reductions, but can apply to plants, processes, technology, financial elements and office locations.

Scope creep: When clients find themselves overly involved in tangential aspects of a project.

Shareholder value: The total net wealth of a company's stockholders. The primary goal of consultants in undertaking most engagements is to maximize shareholder value.

Silo: The tendency of a firm to emphasize vertical relationships within the organization at the expense of horizontal (interdepartmental, etc.) ones.

Six Sigma: A process used by consultants to measure a company's performance. The term comes from the notion that a company's performance metric should never be more than six standard deviations (sigmas) from the ideal.

Stakeholder: A person who has a stake in the outcome of a particular situation. Most commonly, the stakeholders in a case are the shareholders, creditors or employees.

Supply chain: The means and process of physically distributing goods to the consumer.

Total quality management (TQM): Management with the purpose of producing a product or service of the highest quality, with zero tolerance for defects.

Up or out: A promotion policy that requires consultants to leave a firm if not promoted within a certain period of time (usually two to three years). Also known as "sink or swim."

Value-based management: A consulting strategy whose ultimate goal is to increase shareholder value for the client.

Value migration: The flow of economic and shareholder value away from obsolete business models to new, more effective designs.

Value-added: Used to define a service or product in a marketplace that adds value to a preexisting product or way of doing things.

Venture capital: A particular form of private equity (i.e., equity in privately-held businesses) where the funded entity is a new, early-stage business venture.

Work plan: A schedule for completing a consulting engagement.

White paper: A report whose goal is to educate consumers on a major issue.

White space opportunity: An opportunity for a company to make money in an area in which it currently generates zero revenue (for example, launching a new product line, licensing an existing brand or technology, or entering a new geographic market).

Writing a deck: Preparing slides for presentations to clients.

About the Authors

Laura Walker Chung: Laura was formerly a partner in a boutique management consulting firm in Boston, where she specialized in marketing science applications for the life sciences industry. Previously, she gained consulting experience in a 500-person health care strategy boutique, a 100-person energy economics boutique and a 50,000-person generalist firm. She is also the author of The *Vault Career Guide to the Energy Industry*. Laura and Eric currently live in Portland, Oregon, where Laura is applying her consulting skills in the startup world. Laura is a 1995 summa cum laude graduate of Dartmouth College and a 2001 graduate of the University of Chicago Graduate School of Business.

Eric Chung: Having spent his childhood as a quant jock and later as a theoretical physics major in college, Eric is now applying his analytical skills to a career in management consulting. Eric continues to enjoy a long and thrilling run managing projects with Strategic Decisions Group, a boutique consultancy based in Palo Alto, California. He specializes in solving strategy problems for U.S. and international clients using decision analysis methodologies. In his spare time, he is an active singer/songwriter. Eric is also the co-author of The *Vault Guide to the Consulting Case Interview*. He is a 1996 graduate of Harvard College and a 2001 graduate of the University of Chicago Graduate School of Business.

GO FOR THE GOLD!

GET VAULT GOLD MEMBERSHIP AND GET ACCESS TO ALL OF VAULT'S AWARD-WINNING CONSULTING CAREER INFORMATION

- ◆ **Employee surveys** for top consulting firms, with insider info on
  - Company culture
  - Salaries and compensation
  - Hiring process and interviews
  - Business outlook

- ◆ Access to **100+ extended insider consulting firm profiles**

- ◆ **Vault's exclusive consulting firm rankings**, including quality of life and practice area rankings

- ◆ Insider consulting salary information with **Vault's Consulting Salary Central**

- ◆ **Student and alumni surveys** for 100s of top MBA programs and law schools

- ◆ Access to **complete Vault message board archives**

- ◆ **15% off** all Vault purchases, including Vault Guides, Consulting Employer Profiles and Case Interview Prep

For more information go to
www.vault.com/consulting

VAULT
> the most trusted name in career informa